The Spirit Within

COOKING WITH FERMENTED AND DISTILLED BEVERAGES

Happy Cooking!

Karen Burrell

Karen Burrell

ISBN: 1451556861

ISBN-13: 9781451556865

Library of Congress Catalog Number: 2010908213

Table of Contents

Thank you

I thank my Creator for the opportunities that lead to this project.

I thank my mother, Arlene Scheloske, for teaching me to cook and how to read a recipe.

I thank my sister, Debra Eggers, for the kick in the pants to keep it moving.

I thank my cousin, Petra McDaniel, for her enthusiasm.

I thank my husband, James (J. Dee) Burrell, for letting me try new things.

I thank you for purchasing my book. I wish for you many years of flavorful meals, filled with laughter, among family and friends.

Please purchase more copies to give as gifts.

Words of Wisdom

A cheerful heart is good medicine,
but a crushed spirit dries up the bones.

Proverbs 17:22

EQUIVALENT MEASURES

3 teaspoon (tsp)	= 1 Tablespoon	
2 Tablespoons	= 1 ounce	
4 Tablespoons	= 1/4 cup	= 2 ounces
8 Tablespoons	= ½ cup	= 4 ounces
5 1/3 Tablespoons	= 1/3 cup	= 5 ounces
12 Tablespoons	= 3/4 cup	= 6 ounces
16 Tablespoons	= 1 cup	= 8 ounces
2 cups	= 1 pint	= 16 ounces
2 pints	= 1 quart	= 32 ounces
4 cups	= 1 quart	
4 quarts	= 1 gallon (liquid)	= 128 ounces

	Amount	Approx. Measure
Butter	1 pound	2 cups
Butter	1 stick	½ cup
Cheddar Cheese	4 ounces	1 cup shredded
Chocolate Chips	6 ounces	1 cup
Flour	1 pound	3/1/2 - 4 cups
Lemon	medium	2 - 3 Tablespoons juice
Lemon	medium	1 ½ - 3 tsp lightly grated peel
Orange	medium	1/3 - ½ cup juice
Orange	medium	1 - 2 Tablespoons lightly grated peel
Sugar - Brown	1 pound	2 1/4 cups - firmly packed
Sugar - Confectioners'	1 pound	about 4 cups
Sugar - granulated	1 pound	2 1/4 cups

NON-ALCOHOLIC SUBSTITUTIONS

Remember - it will not taste the same.

Alcohol Ingredient	Substitute - General	Substitute Measured
Amaretto	Non-alcoholic almond extract	For 2 Tablespoons amaretto, substitute 1/4 to ½ teaspoon almond extract
Beer or Ale	Chicken broth, white grape juice or ginger ale	
Bourbon	Non-alcoholic vanilla extract; Sparkling apple cider, sparkling cranberry juice, or	For 2 Tablespoons bourbon, substitute 1 - 2 tsp vanilla extract
Brandy	Raspberry extract; water, white grape juice, or apple juice	2 Tablespoons brandy, substitute ½ - 1 tsp raspberry extract
Champagne	Ginger Ale or soda water	
Kirsch	Syrup or juice from black cherries, raspberries, boysenberries, currants, or grapes	
Cognac	Juice from peaches, apricots or pears	
Coffee Liqueur	Espresso or coffee syrup	
Creme de Cacao	Powdered white chocolate mixed with water or non-alcoholic vanilla extract and powdered sugar	

Creme de Cassis	Black currant jam	
Creme de Menthe	Non-alcoholic mint extract, or spearmint extract, or oil of spearmint diluted with a little water or grapefruit juice	
Grand Marnier	Unsweetened orange juice concentrate, orange zest, orange juice, or marmalade	For 2 Tablespoons Grand Marnier substitute 2 Tablespoons orange juice and ½ tsp orange extract or 2 Tablespoons Orange juice concentrate
Peppermint Schnapps	Non-alcoholic mint extract, or mint leaves	
Rum	Non-alcoholic vanilla or rum extract, or pineapple juice or syrup flavored with almond extract	For 2 Tablespoons rum, substitute ½ to 1 tsp rum extract, or 2 Tablespoons water, white grape juice or apple juice
Sherry	Apple cider, non-alcoholic vanilla extract, coffee, or coffee syrup	For 2 Tablespoons sherry, substitute 1 - 2 tsp vanilla extract, or 2 Tablespoon orange or pineapple juice
Vermouth	Apple cider, or apple juice mixed with lemon juice and water	
Vodka	Water, apple cider, or white grape juice mixed with lime juice	

Wine - Riesling	White grape juice mixed with water and a pinch of powdered sugar	
Wine - Gewurztraminer	White grape juice mixed with lemon juice, water, and a pinch of powdered sugar	
Wine - white	White grape juice, chicken broth, vegetable broth	
Wine -white, dry	Water, chicken broth, bullion, consomme, ginger ale, white grape juice, diluted cider vinegar	
Wine - red	red grape juice, cranberry juice, apple cider, chicken broth	

Why cook with alcohol?

Alcohol causes many foods to release flavors that cannot be experienced without the alcohol interaction. Beer contains yeast which leavens breads and batters. Some alcoholic beverages can help break down tough fibers via marinades.

Research suggests that moderate amounts of alcohol can raise your good cholesterol and thin your blood. Wine reduces the risk of heart disease, certain cancers and slows the progression of neurological degenerative disorders like Alzheimer's and Parkinson's Disease.

Not ALL of the alcohol disappears or evaporates during cooking.

Preparation Method	Alcohol Retained
Alcohol added to boiling liquid, and removed from heat	85%
Alcohol flamed	75%
No heat, stored overnight	70%
Baked, 25 minutes, alcohol not stirred into mixture	45%
Baked or simmered, alcohol stirred into mixture:	
15 minutes	40%
30 minutes	35%
1 hour	25%
1.5 hours	20%
2 hours	10%
2.5 hours	5%

Keep in mind that this is the percentage of alcohol remaining of the original addition. If you use 100 proof rum, for example, it is 50% alcohol by volume.

If you bake or simmer the dish for 1 hour, the dish will have 2 percent alcohol content in the entire dish. Divide that by the number of servings and the quantity goes down proportionately.

WHAT'S THE DIFFERENCE?

Bourbon vs. Whiskey (Whisky)

All bourbons are whiskey, but not all whiskeys are bourbon. Whiskey or whisky spelling depends, somewhat, on what part of the world is spelling it. Canadians and Scots spell it "whisky". The Irish spell it "whiskey". Most U.S. dictionaries use "whiskey", but the U.S. Standards of Identity for Distilled Spirits spells it "whisky". For whiskey to qualify as bourbon, it must be made in the USA.

There is a big difference between Kentucky Bourbon and Tennessee Whiskey, so there are recipes for both, here. It's interesting to read about the differences, but I'd rather use the space for more recipes, so if you want to learn more, Google it.

Bourbon should add a very faint flavor of caramel, vanilla, charcoal, and a very light taste of wood to your recipes. These flavors work well in both savory and sweet dishes.

Liqueur vs. Liquor

In general, liqueurs are spirits sweetened with various flavors, oils and extracts. Liqueur alcohol content can range from 15% to 55%, so potency is not a distinguishing factor. Rum, whiskey, brandy and other liquors can serve as the base spirit for liqueurs.

Cream liqueurs have cream added, while creme liqueurs are much sweeter.

Liquor is a spirit made of grains or other plants which are fermented. Sugar is generally used in the fermentation process, but the resulting liquor is not sugary sweet.

Light Brown Sugar vs. Dark Brown Sugar

Dark brown sugar has more molasses in it. Use whichever you prefer.

LIQUOR STORAGE TIPS

1. Keep opened bottles sealed tightly. Use the original cap or a replacement cork.
2. Never store liquor bottles with speed pourers attached unless they are in use.
3. Avoid exposure to extreme hot or cold temperatures.
4. Store your liquor away from exterior walls.
5. Avoid exposing your liquor to any type of sunlight or bright lighting.

The shelf life of most distilled liquors is almost indefinite when unopened. Some variations, such as liqueurs, have a very short shelf life. Under the proper storage conditions, distilled spirits can last a very long period of time opened.

Brandy, gin, rum, tequila, vodka, and whiskey are the most stable distilled spirits and can be stored from several months to several years.

Liqueurs contain sugar, sweeteners or other ingredients that can spoil or go bad. Most opened liqueurs should last for several months or longer depending on their percentage of alcohol content and the type and amount of preservatives. If there are any signs of sugar crystallizing on the bottom, discoloration, curdling or other similar changes, you will need to discard it. Cream liqueurs that contain dairy, cream or egg products should be consumed by their expiration date.

Vermouth can be stored in an open bottle for at least a few months. It will lose most of its flavor if stored too long after opening.

Any beer drinker will tell you that beer is not meant to be stored.

If you open a bottle of wine for cooking, drink the leftovers that day or the next.

Special Beverages

Do not forget to entertain strangers,
for by so doing some people have entertained
angels without knowing it.

Hebrews 13:2

DELUXE KIR ROYALE

1 1/4 cups frozen unsweetened blackberries, thawed (about 5 oz)
4 Tablespoons creme de cassis
1 750-ml bottle chilled Champagne or other sparkling wine

Puree berries in processor. Press puree through sieve into small bowl; discard seeds. Spoon 1 Tablespoon berry puree and 1 Tablespoon creme de cassis into each of 4 Champagne flutes. Fill each flute with Champagne and serve.
4 servings.

CREME DE MENTHE SHAKE

1 quart vanilla ice cream, softened
½ cup green creme de menthe
1/4 cup Irish cream liqueur

In blender container, combine all ingredients. Blend on high speed for 1 minute or until smooth. Makes 10 (½ cup) servings.

BATHTUB GIN FIZZ

2 (2-liter) bottles lemon-lime soda
1 (12 oz) can frozen lemonade concentrate, thawed
½ cup lime juice
1/4 cup confectioners'sugar
2 1/4 cups gin
Ice

In large punch bowl, combine soda, lemonade concentrate, lime juice and powdered sugar. Stir to blend. Gently stir in gin. Serve over ice.

CHAMPAGNE NECTAR PUNCH

2 (12 oz) cans apricot nectar
1 (6 oz) can frozen orange juice concentrate
3 cups water
1/4 cup lemon juice
1/8 tsp salt
3 (4/5) bottles champagne, chilled

Mix all ingredients except champagne. Chill. Add champagne just before serving.

CRANBERRY PUNCH

1 (750 ml) bottle cranberry liqueur, chilled
1 (750 ml)) bottle light rum, chilled
2 (32 oz) bottles club soda, chilled
1 cup lemon juice, chilled
ice
Peaches, strawberries, and oranges, sliced

Combine cranberry liqueur, rum, club soda, and lemon juice in punch bowl. Add ice. Garnish with fruit.

HOT BUTTERED RUM

1 lb brown sugar
½ cup butter, softened
1/4 tsp nutmeg
½ tsp cinnamon
½ tsp cloves
Rum

Cream sugar and butter. Add spices to make base. In a 6-oz mug, put 1 jigger rum and 1 heaping tablespoon of base mixture. Fill with boiling water. Base keeps in refrigerator for months.

FRUIT PUNCH

6 lemons
4 oranges
1 oz brandy
1 oz rum
1 pint strawberries (frozen OK)
2 qt white wine
3 pints Club Soda
1 oz sherry
dash - Curacao
sugar to taste

Juice citrus, reserving several slices for floating in punch. Puree strawberries. Pour wine into punch bowl. Add brandy, rum, sherry, Curacao, and fruit juices. Sweeten as needed. Float citrus slices. Just before serving, add Club Soda.

ORANGE PUNCH

1 (6oz) can frozen orange juice concentrate
1 (6 oz) can frozen lemonade concentrate
2 cups cold water
3 cups white wine
1 cup orange liqueur
1 28 oz bottle of lemon-lime soda
Ice
orange slices

In punch bowl, combine frozen concentrates and water. Mix until smooth. Stir in wine and orange liqueur. Add soda and ice. Stir gently. Top with orange slices.

KAHLUA PARTY PUNCH

2 cups Kahlua, chilled
1 (12 oz) can frozen apple juice concentrate, thawed
½ cup lemon juice, chilled
1 (25.5 oz) bottle sparkling apple juice, chilled
1 (32 oz) bottle lemon-lime soda, chilled
1 (750 ml) bottle dry Champagne, chilled
1 lemon, thinly sliced
1 orange, thinly sliced
chunk ice

In medium bowl, combine Kahlua, apple juice concentrate and lemon juice. Pour over chunk ice in punch bowl. Add sparkling apple juice, then lemon-lime soda. Add Champagne and stir gently. Garnish with fruit slices.

NEW YEAR'S COCKTAIL

3 cups cranberry juice cocktail
1 cup peach schnapps
1 cup vodka

Combine all ingredients in 1 ½ qt. container. Stir to blend. Cover and refrigerate until ready to serve. Serve over crushed ice.
Makes about six 6 oz. servings.

PEPPERMINT-RUM PUNCH

1 (46 oz) can pineapple juice
2 cups water
1 cup peppermint schnapps
1 (12 oz) can frozen limeade concentrate, thawed
1 cup rum
24 oz chilled lemon-lime soft drink

Mix all ingredients in 1-gallon container. Tint green, if desired. Store in refrigerator. Serve over ice.

SANGRIA SPRITZER

2 cups boiling water
6 tea bags
1 qt. apple cider
1 (750 ml) bottle dry white wine
2 (6 oz) cans frozen orange juice concentrate, thawed
2 (6 oz) cans frozen lemonade concentrate, thawed
2 (7 oz) bottles club soda, chilled
lemon and apple slices

In teapot, pour boiling water over tea bags. Cover and brew 5 minutes. Remove tea bags and cool slightly. In punch bowl, combine concentrates, wine, cider, and tea. Refrigerate, covered, until chilled. Just before serving, add club soda. Serve with ice and garnish with lemon and apple slices.

SPICED FRUIT PUNCH

½ cup water
1/3 cup sugar
4 cinnamon sticks, broken
12 whole cloves
4 cups apple juice, chilled
1 (12 oz) can apricot nectar, chilled
1/4 cup lemon juice
2 (750 ml) bottles dry white wine, chilled
orange slices, quartered

In saucepan, combine water, sugar, and spices. Bring to boil. Reduce heat. Cover and simmer for 10 minutes. Remove from heat. Cool. Chill in refrigerator, covered, for at least 2 hours. Strain spices from mixture. Add fruit juices to mixture. Pour into punch bowl and add wine. Garnish with orange slices.

SUNNY CHAMPAGNE PUNCH

2 (46 oz) cans pineapple juice
2 (750 ml) bottles dry Champagne, chilled
2 cups Chenin blanc wine, chilled
1 (20 oz) can chunk pineapple in juice
ice cubes
1 lemon, thinly sliced
1 orange, thinly sliced

In large punch bowl, combine pineapple juice, Champagne, wine and undrained pineapple chunks. Add ice cubes. Float lemon and orange slices on top.

STRAWBERRY SPRITZERS

3 cups strawberries, cut in half
1/4 cup Grand Marnier
1 (750 ml) bottle dry white wine, chilled
1 (1 liter) bottle sparkling water, chilled

In blender, mix strawberries and Grand Marnier. Cover and blend on high speed about 30 seconds or until smooth. Pour about 3 Tablespoons strawberry mixture over crushed ice in each of 8 glasses. Stir about 1/3 cup wine and ½ cup sparkling water into each glass.

HOT SPICED WINE

1 qt. water
2 cups sugar
25 whole cloves
3 cinnamon sticks
½ lemon, peeled
1 (1.5L) bottle Zinfandel

In medium saucepan, combine water, sugar, spices and lemon. Boil over medium-high heat until mixture is syrupy. Reduce heat to low. Add wine; simmer 5 minutes. Do not let wine boil. Strain through a fine sieve, and serve hot.

Appetizers

Our mouths were filled with laughter, our tongues with songs of joy. Then it was said among the nations, "The Lord has done great things for them." The Lord has done great things for us, and we are filled with joy.

Psalm 126:2-3

TERIYAKI CHICKEN WINGS

3 lbs chicken wings (about 20 wings)
½ cup catsup
1/4 cup dry white wine
1/4 cup soy sauce
2 Tablespoons sugar
1 tsp salt
½ tsp ground ginger
1 clove garlic, crushed

Cut each chicken wing at joint to make 3 pieces. Discard tips. Place chicken in ungreased baking dish, 13x9x2 inches. In bowl, mix remaining ingredients. Pour over chicken. Cover and refrigerate about 1 hour, turning occasionally.

Heat over to 375 degrees. Drain chicken, reserving marinade. Place chicken on rack in aluminum foil lined broiler pan. Bake 30 minutes. Brush with reserved marinade. Turn chicken; bake, brushing occasionally with marinade, until tender, 30-40 minutes.
8-12 servings

PORT CHEDDAR CHEESE SPREAD

1 lb. Sharp Cheddar cheese, shredded
1/4 cup butter, softened
1/4 cup sour cream
2 Tablespoons port wine
1/4 tsp ground mace
1/8 tsp ground red pepper
1 cup walnuts, chopped and toasted
veggies or crackers

In bowl, combine sour cream, wine, mace, and ground red pepper. Add butter. Add cheese. Move to food processor. Cover and process until smooth. Mix in walnuts. Refrigerate, covered, several days to allow flavors to mellow. Soften slightly at room temperature before serving. Serve with assorted veggies and crackers.

SAVORY CHEESE SPREAD

8 oz. Sharp Cheddar Cheese, shredded
8 oz. Muenster cheese, shredded
8 oz. Swiss cheese, shredded
1 cup sour cream
½ cup white wine
1 tsp Worcestershire sauce
1 tsp Tabasco sauce
1/4 tsp salt
1/4 tsp ground pepper
1/4 tsp garlic powder

In small mixing bowl, combine all ingredients, except cheeses. In large mixing bowl, mix together cheeses. Mix in sauce. In blender or food processor, process smooth. Store, covered in refrigerator until ready to use. Let stand at room temperature 20-30 minutes or until soft enough to spread. Serve with crackers or bread.

BEER CHEESE SPREAD

1 lb aged natural cheddar cheese, grated finely
1 lb natural Swiss cheese, grated finely
1 clove garlic, mashed
1 tsp dry mustard
1 - 2 tsp Worcestershire sauce
1 cup beer

In bowl, mix cheeses. Mix in garlic. Stir together the dry mustard and Worcestershire and then add to mix. Gradually mix in the beer until the mixture is well blended and of spreading consistency.

Store in a covered container in refrigerator. Serve at room temperature.
Makes 1 quart.

GRAND MARNIER FRUIT SALAD

3 Tablespoons lime juice
1/4 cup confectioners' sugar
3 Tablespoons Grand Marnier
2 Tablespoons apricot jam
1 can mandarin orange sections, drained
1 cup seedless grapes, cut in half lengthwise
1 cup strawberries, hulled, cut bite-size
1 cup blueberries
1 mango, peeled and diced to 1-inch cubes
1 apple, diced
1 pear, peeled, diced
1 cup miniature marshmallows (optional)

In small bowl, combine lime juic, sugar, Grand Marnier, and apricot jam. Whisk to combine.

In large bowl, mix the fruits and marshmallows. Drizzle with Grand Marnier dressing and gently toss to coat.

Refrigerate for 1 hour before serving.

Serves 8

BEER CHEESE DIP

2 (8oz) packages cream cheese, softened
1 package (3 Tablespoons) ranch dressing mix
2 cups shredded sharp Cheddar cheese
2 green onions - tops only, chopped
1/3 - ½ cup beer

In bowl, combine cream cheese and ranch dressing. Stir in cheese and green onions. Stir in beer to desired consistency.
Cover and refrigerate overnight.

KAHLUA PICADILLO

1/4 cup raisins, finely chopped
4 Tablespoons Kahlua, divided
1/3 cup onion, finely chopped
1 Tablespoon oil
1 tsp salt
1/8 tsp pepper
1 lb. ground chuck
1 (14.5 oz) can tomatoes, chopped
½ cup canned green chilies, finely chopped
2 Tablespoons vinegar, divided
1/3 cup pine nuts
Taco Chips

In small bowl, combine raisins and 3 Tablespoons Kahlua; set aside. In large skillet, heat oil. Cook and stir onion over medium-high heat until onion is transparent. Remove from heat. Add chilies, 1 Tablespoon of vinegar, the salt and pepper. Add beef and raisin mixture; mix thoroughly. Return to heat. Lightly brown meat over medium heat, breaking up meat as it cooks. Drain and discard fat. Add tomatoes and remaining 1 Tablespoon each of Kahlua and vinegar. Bring to a boil over high heat. Reduce heat to low; simmer, uncovered, until thickened, about 15 minutes. Stir in nuts. Serve with taco chips.

SESAME PORK APPETIZERS

1 ½ lbs. pork tenderloin
½ cup + 1 Tablespoon dry sherry, divided
⅓ cup + 1 Tablespoon soy sauce, divided
½ cup honey
½ cup sesame seeds
1 Tablespoon sesame oil
1 garlic clove, crushed
spinach leaves for garnish
½ tsp ginger, grated
1 green onion, finely chopped

Place pork in large plastic bag. Combine ½ cup of the sherry and 1 Tablespoon of the soy sauce; pour over pork, turning to coat. Seal bag. Marinate in refrigerator 1-2 hours, turning several times.

Preheat oven to 350 degrees.

Remove pork from marinade. Discard marinade. Spread honey on plate. Roll pork in honey, then in sesame seeds. Arrange pork on roasting rack set in roasting pan. Bake for 25-30 minutes or until meat thermometer registers 155 degrees. Let stand 5 minutes. Slice thinly on the diagonal. Set aside.

Combine remaining 1/3 cup soy sauce, remaining 1 Tablespoon sherry, the sesame oil, garlic, ginger and onion in small bowl. Place bowl in center of serving platter.   Surround the bowl with spinach leaves. Arrange pork slices on top of leaves.

MARINATED VEGETABLE MEDLEY

1 medium broccoli bunch, cut into florets
1 medium cauliflower head, cut into florets
1 small red onion, sliced, rings separated
1 small green bell pepper, cut into strips, seed removed
1 cup vegetable oil
⅔ cup dry white wine
1 Tablespoon Dijon mustard
½ tsp dried dill weed, crushed
1 tsp salt
1 tsp sugar
1/8 tsp pepper

In large plastic bag, combine vegetables. In medium bowl, combine remaining ingredients. Pour over vegetable; toss to coat. Seal bag. Marinate in refrigerator 1 - 2 days, turning bag over occasionally. Remove vegetable with slotted spoon before serving.

CAJUN BEER-BATTERED ONION RINGS

3 large sweet onions (Vidalia or Spanish), peeled and cut into rings
2 1/4 cups flour
2 tsp cajun seasoning OR 1/4 tsp cayenne pepper
2 tsp baking powder
1 tsp salt
1/4 cup cornmeal
2 cups beer (light colored beer)
1 large egg, lightly beaten
oil - for frying

Place the onion rings in a large bowl of ice water. Let stand for 35 minutes. Drain and place on paper towels. Pat dry. Dry WELL to prevent oil splattering.

In large bowl, combine flour, seasoning, baking powder, salt and cornmeal. Mix well. Add the beer and egg to mixture. Stir to blend and smooth. Chill for 20 minutes.
Heat 2 inches oil in a Dutch oven to 375 degrees. Dip onion rings into the batter, coating well. Drop a few onion rings at a time into hot oil and fry until golden brown. Remove with tongs to paper towels to drain. Serve immediately.
Serves 6- 8

CHEESE BALLS

2 packages (8oz each) cream cheese, softened
1 package (4 oz) blue cheese, crumbled
1 cup shredded sharp Cheddar cheese (about 4 oz)
1 Tablespoon brandy
1 tsp instant minced onion
1 cup finely chopped nuts

Mix all ingredients, except nuts. Cover and refrigerate at least 3 hours. Shape mixture into 2 balls. Roll in nuts. To store, wrap in plastic wrap and refrigerate no longer than 2 weeks. Or freeze, no longer than 4 weeks. Thaw wrapped cheese ball in refrigerator about 24 hours before serving.
Makes two 4-inch balls.

Breads

This is the day that the LORD has made;
let us be glad and rejoice in it.

Psalm 118:24

IRISH CREAM MUFFINS

2 eggs, beaten
½ cup sugar
1 tsp vanilla
3/4 cup vegetable oil
3/4 cup Irish Cream
3/4 cup flour
1 ½ tsp baking powder
1/4 cup dried cranberries
1/4 cup chocolate chips

Preheat oven to 400 degrees. Line muffin tin with paper liners.

In large mixing bowl, beat eggs. Gradually add the vanilla and sugar. Beat until frothy. Gradually stir in oil and Irish Cream. Mix flour and baking powder together and stir into sugar mixture. Stir in cranberries and chocolate chips.
Divide equally into the 12 muffin cups. Bake for about 20 minutes or until tester comes out clean. Cool.

FROSTING:

½ cup powdered sugar
4 Tablespoons Irish Cream
Stir together and spread on muffin tops.

MAPLE MERLOT BREAD

1 Tablespoon yeast
2 cups warm half-and-half
2 cups warm red merlot wine
3/4 cup plus 2 Tablespoons maple syrup
1 stick butter, melted
9 cups flour
3/4 cup packed brown sugar
1 ½ Tablespoons salt
1 cup Monterey Jack cheese, shredded

In large bowl, dissolve yeast in the half-and-half. Let stand 5 minutes, until the yeast is foamy. Add the merlot, 3/4 cup maple syrup (not the extra 2 T) and the butter.

In another extra large bowl combine the flour, brown sugar and salt. Mix with a wire whisk. Slowly add the wet ingredients to the dry ingredients and mix well.
Roll out onto a floured countertop or board, and knead for 4 minutes. (Quickly wash and butter the extra-large bowl to reuse for the bread to rise) Put the dough into the well buttered bowl. Cover with dry, clean dish towel. Put in warm, dry, place to rise for 60 minutes.

Generously butter two 9-inch loaf pans.

Punch down the dough with your fist and separate into two portions. Form each loaf and place in pans. Make a deep cut, almost to the pan, in each loaf. In each slash, pack 1 Tablespoon of the maple syrup and ½ cup of the Monterey Jack cheese. Close and smooth the top of the bread.
Cover the pans with the cloth. Place in warm, dry place and let rise for 45-60 minutes.

Preheat over to 400 degrees. Bake for about 1 hour. Check for doneness.
Remove a loaf from the pan and tap the bottom. It should sound hollow, if done. If bread sticks to pan, slide a sharp knife along the edges of the pan and gently nudge the loaf. If not done, return to pan and oven and check every few minutes. When done, cool in the pan for 30 minutes. Remove to cooling rack and cool another 30 minutes before slicing.

BEER AND CHEDDAR MUFFINS

2 Tablespoons unsalted butter, melted
1 1/4 cup cornmeal
3/4 cup flour
2 Tablespoons sugar
1 Tablespoon baking powder
1/2 tsp cayenne pepper
1 small onion, minced
1 egg
1 cup beer
1 ½ cup grated cheddar cheese

Preheat oven to 400 degrees. Grease or paper line muffin tin.
In large mixing bowl, combine flour, cornmeal, sugar, baking powder, and cayenne pepper. In medium bowl, beat egg. Add beer and melted butter. Mix. Make a well in center of dry ingredients and pour in the beer mixture. Stir briskly to combine. Don't over-stir - batter should be lumpy. Stir in cheese. Fill muffin cups 2/3 full. Bake 20 - 25 minutes. Remove from pan onto cooling rack.

BEER BREAD

3 cups flour (sifted)
3 tsp baking powder
1 tsp salt
1/4 cup sugar
1 (12oz) can beer
1/4 cup butter, melted

Preheat oven to 375 degrees. Grease loaf pan.

Mix dry ingredients. Add beer. Stir to mix. Pour into loaf pan. Pour melted butter over mixture. Bake 1 hour. Remove from pan to cooling rack. Cool at least 15 minutes before slicing.

WHISKEY SODA BREAD

1 cup raisins
½ cup Irish whiskey
3 cups flour
½ cup sugar
1 Tablespoon baking powder
1 tsp salt
1 Tablespoon grated orange rind
½ tsp baking soda
1 ½ cups buttermilk
1/4 cup butter, melted

Soak raisins in whiskey overnight.

Preheat oven to 350 degrees. Grease 2-quart casserole.

In large bowl, combine flour sugar, baking powder, salt and orange rind. Mix well. Stir in raisins and remaining soaking whiskey. Blend well. Dissolve soda in buttermilk. Add to flour mixture. Stir well. Stir in butter. Spoon batter into prepared casserole. Bake for 50 minutes or until golden brown. Cut into squares. Serve with Whiskey Butter.

Whiskey Butter:

½ cup butter, softened
1 Tablespoon Irish whiskey

Combine butter and whiskey, blending well.

RUM-RAISIN BANANA BREAD

(bourbon can be substituted for the rum)

1 cup raisins
6 Tablespoons rum
3 cups flour
1 tsp baking powder
1 tsp baking soda
1 tsp salt
1 stick butter, softened
1 cup sugar
2 eggs, slightly beaten
$^1/_3$ cup milk
1 cup mashed ripe banana (about 2 large bananas)
$^1/_2$ cup chopped walnuts

Soak the raisins in the rum at least 30 minutes (or several hours, covered). Stir occasionally.

Preheat oven to 350 degrees. Grease and flour two 9 x 5-inch loaf pans.

Combine flour, baking powder, baking soda, and salt. Set aside. In large mixing bowl, stir together the butter, sugar, eggs, milk, mashed banana, walnuts, and raisins with their rum. Add the dry ingredients and beat just until the batter is thoroughly blended.

Spread evenly in the prepared pans and bake for about 1 hour, or until tester comes out clean. Remove from the oven and let cool in the pans for 5 minutes. Turn out onto a rack to cool.

BEER PUFFS TO FILL

1 cup beer
1 stick of butter
1 cup all-purpose flour
½ tsp salt
4 eggs
filling of your choice; i.e. chicken salad, tuna salad,
or desserts such as mousse

Preheat oven to 450 degrees. Line baking sheets with parchment paper.

In a large heavy saucepan, heat beer and butter until it barely comes to a boil and the butter is melted. Add flour and salt, lower heat, and stir constantly until mixture pulls away from the side of the pan and forms a ball. Remove from the heat and let rest for 1 minute. Add eggs, one at a time, beating each one in until the dough is shiny.

Drop dough in 1-inch rounds onto prepared baking sheets. Bake 10 minutes. Reduce heat to 350 degrees and turn baking sheets. Bake puffs an additional 10 minutes until brown and dry. Turn off oven, crack open the oven door, and let puffs dry further until cool.

Split beer puffs with a fork (or slice with a serrated knife) and fill.
Makes 60-80 small puffs.

RYE BEER BREAD

2 cups rye flour
1 ½ cups beer, room temperature
1 (1/4oz) packages active dry yeast
2 Tablespoons sugar
1 Tablespoon salt
2 Tablespoons shortening
1 egg
1 Tablespoon caraway seed (optional)
3 cups bread flour
1 Tablespoons cornmeal

In large bowl, dissolve yeast in beer. Add rye flour. Mix well. Cover bowl with plastic wrap. Set out overnight. Do not refrigerate.

The next day, in a large bowl, beat egg. Beat in sugar, salt and shortening. If using caraway seeds, add here. Mix in the rye dough. Add enough white bread flour to make a soft dough.

Knead on a lightly floured surface until smooth, approximately 10 minutes. Place in a greased bowl, and turn to oil the surface of the dough. Cover with a towel and let rise in warm place about 1 hour, or until doubled.

Sprinkle baking sheet with cornmeal.

Punch down dough, and divide in half. Shape into loaves and place on greased baking sheet, on top of cornmeal. Cover and let rise for 30 minutes.

Preheat oven to 400 degrees. Bake for 30 minutes. Cool on racks.

SAGE & CHEESE BEER BREAD

2 ½ cups flour
1 Tablespoon baking powder
2 Tablespoons sugar
1 ½ tsp baking soda
1 tsp salt
1 ½ tsp dried sage
1 (12oz) can beer
1 cup shredded Cheddar cheese

Preheat oven to 375 degrees. Grease loaf pan.

Mix dry ingredients. Stir in beer and cheese. Mix well. Spread evenly in pan. Bake 50-55 minutes. Cool 10 minutes.

WHOLE WHEAT BEER BREAD

4 ½ tsp baking powder
1 ½ tsp salt
1 ½ cups whole wheat flour
1 ½ cups flour
1/3 cup brown sugar, packed
1 (12oz) can or bottle beer

Preheat oven to 350 degrees. Lightly grease a 9 x 5 inch loaf pan.

In large mixing bowl, combine dry ingredients. Make well in center. Pour in beer. Stir until a stiff batter forms. It may be necessary to mix dough with your hands. Place dough into loaf pan. Bake 50-60 minutes, until tester comes out clean

CRANBERRY CITRUS MUFFIN

2 oz dark rum
1 cup corn syrup
½ oz fresh lemon juice
1/4 cup butter, softened, chopped
2 eggs
2 cups flour
2 tsp baking powder
1/4 tsp salt
½ cup Ruby Tangerine Grapefruit Juice Drink
2 cups frozen cranberry, coarsely chopped

Preheat oven to 350 degrees. Line muffin tin with cup papers.

In medium mixing bowl, combine rum, lemon juice, corn syrup and butter. Beat until light and fluffy. Add eggs, one at a time, beating after each addition.

In another bowl, sift together the flour, baking powder and salt. Alternately, add some dry mix and some juice drink to the butter mixture. Stir in cranberries.

Spoon into muffin cups, filling about 3/4 full. Bake 20 minutes or until golden brown. Makes 12 muffins.

BEER DINNER ROLLS

1 (1/4 oz) package dry yeast
1 cup warm water
2 Tablespoons sugar
1 egg, slightly beaten
2/3 cup milk
1 tsp salt
6 Tablespoons butter, melted, divided
4-5 cups flour
½ cup beer, room temperature

In large bowl, dissolve yeast in warm water. Add sugar, egg, milk, salt, and 2 Tablespoons butter. Gradually add small amounts of flour to mixture, alternating with small amounts of beer. Mix thoroughly after each addition. Dough should be slightly moist. Knead until bubbles appear.

Butter large bowl. Roll dough around in bowl to butter all sides of dough. Cover with clean, dry towel and let rise in a warm place for approximately 1 - 1 ½ hours.

Form rolls. Place on buttered cookie sheet. Cover and let rise in warm place for 1 - 1 ½ hours.

Preheat oven to 475 degrees. Bake until brown. They bake quickly, 12-15 minutes. Makes 30-36 rolls.

RUM-RAISIN CARROT BREAD

1 cup raisins

½ cup rum

1 1/3 cups sugar

1 1/3 cups water

4 Tablespoons butter

1 cup grated raw carrot (about 3 large carrots)

1 tsp salt

2 tsp cinnamon

½ tsp group allspice

1/4 tsp nutmeg

1/4 tsp ground cloves

2 cups flour

1 tsp baking soda

1 tsp baking powder

1 ½ cups chopped walnuts

Soak the raisins in the rum, covered, for 1-6 hours. Stir occasionally.

In a saucepan, combine the sugar, water, butter, carrot, salt, cinnamon, allspice, nutmeg and cloves. Stir well. Bring to a boil and boil for 5 minutes, stirring frequently. Remove from the heat and let cool to tepid (several hours).

Preheat the oven to 350 degrees. Grease and flour a 9 x 5 -inch loaf pan.
In large bowl. Mix the flour, baking soda, and baking powder. Add the carrot mixture. Blend well. Stir in the raisins and walnuts. Spread evenly in the prepared pan and bake for about 1 hour, or until tester comes out clean. Remove from the oven and let cool in the pan for 5 minutes. Turn out onto a cooling rack. Cool completely.

APRICOT ALMOND BREAD

1 cup dried apricots
½ cup Grand Marnier
½ cup water
1 egg, slightly beaten
1 cup sugar
4 Tablespoons butter, melted and cooled
2 cups flour
2 tsp baking powder
1/4 tsp baking soda
1 tsp salt
1 cup chopped almonds.

Cut the apricots into sixths. In a small bowl, soak apricot pieces in the Grand Marnier for 1 hour.

Preheat the oven to 350 degrees. Grease and flour a 9 x 5 inch loaf pan.

In large bowl, mix water, egg, sugar, and butter. Beat until smooth. In separate bowl, combine flour, baking powder, baking soda, and salt. Mix into egg mixture. Beat just until the batter is smooth. Stir in apricots and remaining Grand Marnier and almonds.

Spread evenly in the prepared pan and bake for about 70 minutes, or until the tester comes out clean. Remove from the oven and let cool for about 5 minutes. Turn out onto cooling rack to cool completely. It will be easier to slice if you wrap it airtight and let it sit overnight.

GRAND MARNIER CRANBERRY MUFFINS

1 1/4 cup orange juice
1/4 cup Grand Marnier liqueur
3/4 cup oil
2 cups chopped cranberries
2 ½ cups all-purpose flour
1 cup whole wheat flour
1 ½ cups sugar
2 Tablespoons baking powder
½ tsp salt
1 ½ Tablespoons chopped orange zest
4 egg whites

Preheat oven to 400 degrees. Line 24 muffin cups with paper cups.

In small bowl, combine orange juice, Grand Marnier, and oil. Set aside. In a large bowl, combine the flours, sugar, baking powder, salt and orange zest. In another large bowl, beat the egg whites until frothy. Combine the juice mixture with the beaten egg whites. Add the egg mixture and the cranberries to the flour mixture, stirring just until moist. ivide the batter among the 24 muffin cups. Bake for 25 minutes or until golden brown and puffed.

AMARETTO ALMOND MUFFINS

2/3 cup sour milk
3 Tablespoons melted butter
1 egg, slightly beaten
½ cup amaretto
1 cup sliced almonds
2 tsp baking powder
½ cup sugar
2 cups flour

Preheat oven to 400 degrees. Grease muffin pan.   In mixing bowl, combine milk, butter, egg, amaretto, and almonds. Mix well. Add remaining ingredients; blend. Spoon into muffin pan. Bake for 15 - 20 minutes.

KUGELHUPF

1 package dry yeast
½ cup milk, warmed
½ cup sugar
2 tsp salt
5 eggs
1/4 cup rum
2 tsp vanilla
1 Tablespoon grated orage zest
4 cups flour
1/4 tsp cinnamon
1/4 tsp nutmeg
1 stick butter, softened, chopped
½ cup chopped almonds
1 cup raisins
½ cup sliced almonds

Stir the yeast into the warm milk and let stand to dissolve. In a large bowl, combine the sugar, salt, and eggs. Beat well. Stir in the dissolved yeast. Sift together 2 cups of flour, cinnamon, nutmeg and add to mixture. Add the butter and beat until the batter is smooth and well blended. Add the remaining flour, chopped almonds and raisins. Beat again until smooth. The batter will be very heavy and sticky. Cover the bowl and let rise until double in bulk - maybe 3 hours or more.

Grease the Kugelhupf pan or Bundt pan thoroughly. Punch the dough down and place it in the pan, punching and patting it into place to fit evenly. Cover the pan and let rise until double in bulk.

Preheat the oven to 400 degrees. Press the sliced almonds on the top of the bread. Bake for 10 minutes, then reduce the heat to 350 degrees and continue baking for about 40 minutes. If the top becomes too brown, cover loosely with foil for the last 20 minutes or so. Remove from the oven and let cool in the pan for about 10 minutes. Turn out onto a rack to cool completely.

PEPPER CHEESE BEER BREAD

1 cup flour

1 cup whole wheat flour

6 oz. hot pepper Monterey Jack cheese, shredded

1 tsp sugar

3/4 tsp baking powder

½ tsp baking soda

½ tsp salt

1 cup beer, room temperature

1/3 cup butter, melted

2 eggs, slightly beaten

Preheat oven to 350 degrees. Grease 9 x 5-inch loaf pan.

In medium bowl, stir together flour, whole wheat flour, 1 cup shredded cheese, sugar, baking powder, soda, and salt. Stir in beer, butter, and eggs, just until moistened. Spoon batter into pan. Sprinkle remaining cheese over batter. Bake for 45-55 minutes or until tester comes out clean. Remove from pan. Cool on wire rack 10 minutes. Serve warm.

Soups

May God give you of heaven's dew and of earth's richness -
an abundance of grain and new wine.

Genesis 27:28

APPLE-BEER CHEESE SOUP

3 Tablespoons butter

1 small onion, minced

3 Tablespoons flour

1 1/4 cups chicken broth

3/4 cup unsweetened applesauce

1 (12 oz) can beer, room temperature

1/8 tsp ground nutmeg

1/8 tsp white pepper

dash Worcestershire sauce

salt to taste

4 oz. Swiss cheese, shredded

4 oz. Monterey Jack cheese, shredded

In medium saucepan, melt butter over medium heat. Add onion; cook until softened, stirring occasionally.   Stir in flour; cook until bubbly, stirring constantly. Gradually stir in chicken broth; cook until thickened, stirring constantly. Stir in applesauce; slowly stir in beer. Season with nutmeg, pepper, Worcestershire sauce and salt to taste. Reduce heat to low; simmer 10-15 minutes, stirring occasionally. Add ½ of the cheese; stir until melted. Add remaining cheese; stir until melted. Do not boil.

CREAM OF BROCCOLI SOUP

1 ½ lbs broccoli, trimmed, coarsely chopped (including peeled stems)
1/4 cup water
1 Tablespoon unsalted butter
1 onion, chopped
2 cloves garlic, chopped
1 Tablespoon flour
2 cups low-sodium chicken broth (or vegetable broth)
2 cups milk
½ cup white wine
½ cup heavy cream
1 tsp salt
1/4 tsp pepper

In large saucepan, heat water and butter over medium-high heat until butter is melted. Add the onion and garlic. Cook, stirring occasionally until it is softened but not browned, 4 - 6 minutes. Add the flour and cook 2 minutes.

Pour in the broth, milk and white wine and bring to a simmer. Add the broccoli and cook, stirring occasionally, until the broccoli is tender but not bright green, 5 - 8 minutes. Remove from heat. Puree until the liquid is smooth. Return to pot. Stir in the cream, salt and pepper. Bring soup to a gentle simmer for 3 - 4 minutes.

Serves 4

CORN CHOWDER

2 Tablespoons olive oil
1 onion, finely chopped
1 celery stalk finely chopped
½ tsp ground coriander
1/3 tsp ground cumin
1/8 tsp cayenne pepper
½ cup dry white wine
3 Yukon Gold potatoes, peeled and cut into ½ inch pieces
2 cups chicken broth
1 cup milk
3 cups corn, frozen, thawed
2 oz. Sharp cheddar cheese, grated (about 3/4 cup)
Chopped scallions for garnish

In large saucepan, heat the olive oil. Add onions and celery and cook until soft, about 7 -8 minutes, stirring occasionally. Add spices, cooking for an additional 30 seconds. Add wine and stir. Cook for additional 3 minutes.

Add the potatoes, stock, and milk. Stir. Bring to a boil, reduce heat and simmer until the potatoes are fork tender.

Transfer 2 cups of the soup to a blender and puree. Return to the pan and stir to combine. When serving, top with scallions and cheese.

Serves 6

VEGETABLE CHEESE SOUP

2 large potatoes, finely chopped, rinsed
2 large onions, finely chopped
½ cup carrots, finely chopped
½ cup celery, finely chopped
2 (12oz) cans beer
4 tsp instant chicken bouillon
2 cups shredded Cheddar cheese
1 cup half-and-half
6 drops red pepper sauce
1/8 tsp ground nutmeg
1/4 cup snipped parsley

In 3-quart saucepan, heat vegetables, beer and instant bouillon to boiling; reduce heat. Cover and simmer until vegetables are tender, about 15 minutes. Stir in remaining ingredients, except parsley; heat through. Sprinkle with parsley.

POTATO HAM SOUP

5 large potatoes, peeled and diced
1 ½ cups pre-cooked ham, diced
6 cups chicken broth
1 onion, peeled and chopped
4 Tablespoons butter
3 leeks, sliced, including green parts
1 bay leaf
1 cup heavy cream
½ cup white wine
1 tsp coriander
salt and pepper to taste

Saute onion and leeks in butter until translucent. In large soup pot, combine potatoes, chicken broth, onion, leeks, bay leaf, and coriander. Bring to a boil; reduce heat and simmer for 30 minutes or until potatoes are soft. Remove from heat. Remove bay leaf. Add wine and heavy cream. Puree. Return soup to pot and add the diced ham. Reheat to low simmer.

Desserts

Go, eat your food with gladness, and drink
your wine with a joyful heart.

Ecclesiastes 9:7

FROSTY LATTE SQUARES

2 cups heavy whipping cream
1/4 cup Kahlua
½ cup chocolate-flavored syrup
½ cup butter, softened
1 cup flour
½ cup pecans, finely chopped

Preheat oven to 350 degrees.

In large bowl, combine whipping cream, Kahlua, and chocolate syrup; refrigerate.

In medium bowl, cut butter into flour, using pastry blender or criss-crossing 2 knives, until evenly mixed. Stir in pecans. Press mixture evenly on bottom of ungreased 9 x 9 inch pan. Bake about 15 minutes or until light brown. Cool completely.

Beat whipping cream mixture on high speed until soft peaks form; spread over crust. Cover and freeze at least 4 hours until firm, but no longer than 48 hours. Cut into 3-inch squares. Serve immediately.

TIRAMISU

Hot-Milk Sponge Cake:
1 cup flour
1 tsp baking powder
2 eggs
½ cup milk
2 Tablespoons butter
1 cup sugar

Preheat oven to 350 degrees. Grease and flour a 9 x 9 x 2 inch baking pan. Chill bowl and electric mixer beaters for whipping cream, later.

In bowl, combine flour and baking powder; set aside. In large mixing bowl, beat eggs with electric mixer on high speed for about 4 minutes or until thick. Gradually add sugar, beating on medium speed for 4 - 5 minutes or until light and fluffy. Add the flour mixture; beat on medium-low speed just until combined. In microwave bowl, heat milk and butter until butter melts; stir and add to batter, beating until combined. Pour batter into prepared pan. Bake for 20 -25 minutes or until tester comes out clean. (*Make Syrup while cake is baking.*) Cool cake for 10 minutes in pan. Run knife around sides of pan to loosen cake; invert onto wire rack to remove cake from pan. Cool cake completely. With long serrated knife, slice into 3 layers.

Syrup:
1/3 cup sugar
2 Tablespoons instant coffee crystals
1/3 cup water
2 Tablespoons rum

In small saucepan, combine sugar, coffee crystals and water. Cook over medium heat to boiling. Boil for 1 minute; remove from heat and stir in rum. Cool completely. Divide in thirds.

Filling:
2 (8 oz) packages cream cheese, softened
½ cup confectioners' sugar
1 tsp vanilla
2 oz + ½ oz semi-sweet chocolate, grated

In medium bowl, stir together the cream cheese, confectioners' sugar and vanilla. Stir in the 2 oz..of grated semi-sweet chocolate.

Assembly:
Return bottom layer of cake to the baking pan. Brush layer in pan with 1/3 of syrup and spread with ½ of the filling. Repeat, layering with the second cake layer, 1/3 of the syrup, and remaining filling. Top with the third cake layer; brush with remaining syrup.

Topping:
1 cup whipping cream
2 Tablespoons Kahlua
½ oz. semi-sweet chocolate, grated

In chilled bowl, combine whipping cream and Kahlua. Beat on medium speed until soft peaks form (tips curl). Spread mixture over cake layer; sprinkle with grated chocolate. Refrigerate at least 4 hours before serving.
Makes 12-16 servings.

AMARETTO BROWNIES

2/3 cup slivered almonds, toasted, chopped
8 oz semisweet chocolate chips
1/3 cup + 3 Tablespoons butter, softened, divided
1 1/4 cups flour
1 cup sugar
3 Tablespoons amaretto, divided
1 tsp baking powder
½ tsp salt
2 eggs, slightly beaten
2 cups confectioners' sugar
1 - 2 Tablespoons milk

Preheat oven to 350 degrees. Grease bottom of 13 x 9 inch pan. In microwave bowl, melt chocolate and 1/3 cup butter, stir until smooth. Stir in half of the chopped almonds, flour, sugar, 2 Tablespoons amaretto, baking powder, salt and eggs. Spread in pan. Bake 22-27 minutes or until tester comes out clean. Cool completely.

Frosting: Mix confectioners' sugar, 3 Tablespoons butter and 1 Tablespoon amaretto. Add 1 -2 Tablespoons milk to get desired spreading consistency. Sprinkle remaining ½ of almonds over frosting.

BRANDY APPLE SPICE CAKE

4 cups Granny Smith apples, peeled, coarsely chopped
1/3 - ½ cup brandy
2 cups sugar
½ cup oil
2 eggs
2 cups flour
2 tsp baking soda
2 tsp ground cinnamon
1 tsp salt
1 tsp nutmeg
½ tsp cloves
1 cup chopped nuts
1 cup raisins

Soak chopped apples and raisins in the brandy for at least 1 hour.

Preheat oven to 325 degrees. Grease and flour 9 x 13 x 2 inch pan.

In large mixing bowl, beat the eggs, add the sugar and oil. Beat until well blended. Sift together the flour cinnamon, soda, salt, nutmeg and cloves. Stir flour mixture into oil mixture until blended. Fold in apples, raisins, and nuts.

Pour batter into pan. Bake for 50-55 minutes or until tester comes out clean. Serve warm or cool with whipped cream.

IRISH CREAM PIE

3/4 cup + 2 Tablespoons flour
½ cup butter, softened
1/4 cup confectioners' sugar
1/4 cup finely chopped pecans
2 Tablespoons cocoa

½ cup milk
32 large marshmallows
1/3 cup Irish cream
1 ½ cups heavy whipping cream
grated semisweet baking chocolate

Pie Crust: Preheat oven to 400 degrees. In medium bowl, mix flour, butter, sugar, pecans, and cocoa until soft dough forms. Press firmly and evenly against bottom and sides of ungreased pie plate. Bake 12-15 minutes or until light brown. Cool completely.

Pie Filling: In microwave bowl, combine milk and marshmallows. Microwave for 1 minute. Stir until smooth. Cool in refrigerator about 15 minutes. Fold in Irish cream. In medium bowl, beat whipping cream on high speed until soft peaks form. Fold marshmallow mixture into whipped cream. Spread in pie crust. Sprinkle with chocolate. Cover and refrigerate at least 4 hours until set, but not longer than 48 hours.

GRAND MARNIER RAISIN GINGERBREAD BARS

1/4 cup Grand Marnier
1 cup raisins
2 cups flour
1 ½ cup brown sugar, packed
2 tsp ground cinnamon
1 tsp ground ginger
½ tsp baking soda
½ tsp salt
2 eggs, beaten
1/3 cup molasses
1 stick butter, melted
2 tsp vanilla
8 oz cream cheese, softened
confectioners' sugar for dusting

In zip-lock bag, combine Grand Marnier and raisins. Squeeze out air and seal. Soak the raisins for 1 hour to overnight. Longer is better.
Preheat oven to 375 degrees. Grease a 13 x 9 inch baking pan.

In large bowl, combine flour, brown sugar, cinnamon, ginger, baking soda, and salt.

In second bowl, combine eggs, molasses, butter, vanilla. Mix in cream cheese. Mix well. Stir in dry ingredient mixture, stirring only until blended. Fold in raisins. Spread batter evenly in pan.

Bake until golden around edges, about 20 minutes. Cool completely. Cut into 24 bars and dust with powdered sugar.

MARGARITA PIE

1 ½ cups crushed pretzel sticks
1/4 cup sugar
1 stick butter, melted
1 (14 oz) can sweetened condensed milk
1/3 cup fresh lime juice
2 Tablespoons tequila
2 Tablespoons Triple Sec
1 - 2 drops green food color, optional
1 cup heavy cream, whipped
lime slices for garnish

Crust: Combine pretzels and sugar. Mix with butter. Press into 9-inch buttered pie plate and chill.

Pie Filling: Combine liquids. Fold whipped cream into mixture. Pour into chilled crust and freeze for 3-4 hours or until firm. Garnish each piece with a thin slice of lime before serving.

MOLTEN SPICED CHOCOLATE CABERNET CAKES

4 oz. semi-sweet chocolate chips
1 stick butter
1 Tablespoon Cabernet Sauvignon
1 tsp vanilla
1 cup confectioners sugar
2 eggs
1 egg yolk
6 Tablespoons flour
1/4 tsp ground cinnamon
1/4 tsp ground ginger

Preheat oven to 425 degrees. Butter 4 custard cups. Place on baking sheet.

Microwave chocolate and butter in large bowl on high for 1 minute. Whisk until chocolate is completely melted. Stir in wine, vanilla, and sugar. Whisk in egg and the additional yolk. Stir in flour, cinnamon and ginger. Spoon evenly into prepared dishes.

Bake for 15 minutes or until sides are firm but centers are soft. Remove from oven. Let stand 1 minute. Loosen edges with knife. Invert onto serving plates. Sprinkle with additional confectioners' sugar, if desired.
Makes 4 servings

CHOCOLATE FONDUE

12 oz milk chocolate chips
3/4 cup half and half
1 - 2 Tablespoons kirsch, brandy, Grand Marnier, or Kahlua
Fruit - sliced bananas, apples, peaches, nectarines, plums; whole strawberries, grapes; sections of oranges or grapefruit
Cubed sweet breads or pound cake

In microwave safe bowl, melt chocolate chips and half and half for 25-second intervals, stirring between until melted and smooth. Stir in liqueur. Pour into a fondue pot with a low flame or a heavy, heat-holding ceramic or glass bowl. Arrange fruit and bread around chocolate container, with fondue fork for dipping. Serve immediately.

APPLE CRANBERRY PIE

1 package (15 oz) refrigerated pie crusts
1/4 cup butter
8-10 Granny Smith Apples, peeled and sliced
3 cups fresh whole cranberries
½ cup granulated sugar
1/3 cup all-purpose flour
1/4 cup packed light brown sugar
2 Tablespoons brandy
1 Tablespoon lemon juice
2 tsp vanilla
1 ½ tsp ground cinnamon

Preheat oven to 350 degrees. Line pie pan with one pie crust; prick with fork. Bake 10 minutes. In mixing bowl, combine the sugars, flour, and cinnamon. Add apples and stir to coat. Add cranberries. Stir. Melt butter in large skillet. Add brandy, lemon juice and vanilla. Add apple mixture and stir. Cook until apples and cranberries are soft but not mushy, stirring often to coat apples and cranberries with butter mixture. Fill partially baked pie crust with apple mixture. Top pie with second crust. Press edges together, Press edges together with fork. Cut several slits in top crust. Bake 35-40 minutes or until filling is bubbly.
Serves 6-8

WATERMELON POPSICLE

5 cups seedless watermelon, chopped
2 tablespoons fresh lime juice
3 Tablespoons granulated sugar
1/4 cup water
1/4 cup tequila

In blender, puree all ingredients until smooth. Strain through a fine-mesh sieve into a bowl. Press on solids in sieve to capture as much liquid as possible. Discard solids. Skim off any foam. Pour into popsicle molds. Freeze 30 minutes. Insert sticks. Freeze until firm, about 24 hours.

GRASSHOPPER PIE

Chocolate Cookie Crust
32 large marshmallows
½ cup milk
1/4 cup creme de menthe
3 Tablespoons white creme de cacao
1 ½ cups whipping cream
few drops of green food color, if desired

Chocolate Cookie Crust:

1 ½ cup chocolate wafer crumbs
1/4 cup butter, melted

Mix butter and crumbs, well. Press mixture firmly against bottom and sides of ungreased 9-inch pie plate. Bake 10 minutes. Cool.

Filling:

In microwave-safe bowl, stir together milk and marshmallows. Microwave 1 minute. Stir, until smooth. Refrigerate until thickened; stir in liqueurs.

Beat whipping cream in chilled bowl until stiff. Fold marshmallow mixture into whipped cream. Add food color, if desired. Pour into crust. Refrigerate until set, at least 3 hours.

POACHED PEAR AND RASPBERRY TRIFLE WITH ORANGE CUSTARD

Pears:
1 750-ml bottle Johannisberg Riesling
3/4 cup sugar
3 lbs Anjou pears, peeled, halved, cored
4 whole cloves
½ cup cream sherry
Custard:
10 large egg yolks
2/3 cup sugar
7 Tablespoons cornstarch
4 cups half-and-half
1/4 cup unsalted butter
1 Tablespoon grated orange peel
2 tsp vanilla extract

1 ½ purchased pound cakes (12oz each)
2/3 cup raspberry jam
5 baskets raspberries
2 cups chilled whipping cream
2 Tablespoons sugar

For Pears: In Large saucepan, bring wine and sugar to simmer, stirring until sugar dissolves. Add pears and cloves and bring to boil. Reduce heat, cover and simmer until pears are just tender, turning occasionally, about 25 minutes. Remove pears to a plate to cool. Boil poaching liquid until reduce to 2/3 cup syrup, about 20 minutes. Cool pear syrup. Mix in cream sherry. Thinly slice pears; drain on paper towels.

For Custard: In bowl, whisk yolks, 2/3 cup sugar and cornstarch. In large heavy saucepan, bring half-and-half to simmer. Gradually whisk hot half-and-half into yolk mixture. Return mixture to same saucepan. Whisk over medium heat until custard boils, about 8 minutes. Boil 1 minute, whisking constantly. Remove from heat. Pour into bowl. Add butter, whisk until melted. Whisk in orange peel and vanilla. Chill until cool, whisking occasionally, about 1 hour.

Assembly: Cut cakes crosswise into 1/2-inch-thick slices. Quarter each slice. Arrange enough cake in bottom of 4-quart glass trifle dish or bowl to cover bottom. Brush cake with 1 Tablespoon pear syrup, then spread 2 Tablespoons jam over. Sprinkle with 1 cup raspberries. Spread 1 1/4 cups custard over cake to cover. Top with single layer of sliced pears. Arrange another layer of cake over. Brush with 3 Tablespoons syrup, then spread 4 Tablespoons jam over. Sprinkle with 1 ½ cups berries. Spread 1 ½ cups custard over. Top with single layer of pears. Arrange another cake layer. Brush with 5 Tablespoons syrup, then spread 5 Tablespoons jam over. Sprinkle 1 ½ cups berries over. Spread remaining custard over. Place remaining pears atop dessert.

Cover and chill at least 4 hours or overnight.
To serve: Whip cream and 1 Tablespoons sugar in large bowl to medium peaks. Serve with Trifle.

BANANAS IN RUM

4 bananas, peeled and halved lengthwise
1 Tablespoon lemon juice
1/4 cup honey
1/4 cup rum
2 Tablespoons butter

Preheat oven to 400 degrees. Butter 9 x 9 baking dish.

In small bowl, mix rum and honey. Place bananas in buttered dish. Brush with lemon juice. Pour honey-rum sauce over. Dot with butter. Bake 20 minutes.

HUMMERS

Each Hummer recipe yields 2 servings. Soften ice cream before adding other ingredients. Blend until creamy.

Golden Hummer
1 oz. Galliano
1 oz. white creme de cacao
2 scoops vanilla ice cream

Velvet Hummer
1 oz Triple Sec
1 oz. brown creme de cacao
2 scoops vanilla ice cream

Mint Hummer
1 oz. green creme de menthe
1 oz. white creme de cacao
2 scoops vanilla ice cream

Mocha Hummer
1 oz. Kahlua
1 oz. Creme de cacao
2 scoops vanilla ice cream

Chocolate Chip Hummer
1 oz. brandy
½ oz white creme de cocao
2 scoops chocolate chip ice cream

Alexander Hummer
1 oz. brown creme de cacao
1 oz. brandy
2 scoops vanilla ice cream
Dash of nutmeg

Citrus Hummer
2 oz. brandy
1 scoop lemon ice cream
1 scoop orange sherbert

HERSHEY BAR PIE

1/3 cup milk
2 cups miniature marshmallows
10 oz milk chocolate without almonds
1 cup whipping cream
½ cup slice almonds

graham cracker pie crust

Creme de Cacao Syrup

Chill a medium mixing bowl and beaters of an electric mixer.

In saucepan, heat and stir milk over low heat until steaming. Add marshmallows. Heat and stir over low heat until melted. Add chocolate. Heat and stir until melted. Remove from heat. Cover surface with waxed paper and cool to room temperature.

In the chilled bowl, beat whipping cream on medium speed until soft peaks form. Gradually fold cooled chocolate mixture into whipped cream. Pour into pie crust. Sprinkle with almonds. Freeze.

Creme de Cacao Syrup
½ cup water
1/3 cup sugar
1/4 cup creme de cacao

In small saucepan combine water and sugar. Bring to boiling, stirring to dissolve sugar. Remove from heat. Stir in creme de cacao. Cover and cool. Makes 1 cup.

To serve: let pie stand a few minutes, cut into wedges, and drizzle each serving with syrup.

BOURBON CARROT CAKE WITH BOURBON GLAZE

2 eggs
2/3 cup oil
1 cup sugar
1 cup flour
1tsp baking powder
1 tsp baking soda
½ tsp salt
½ tsp cinnamon
1/4 tsp nutmeg
3 Tablespoons bourbon
1 ½ cup grated carrots
½ cup raisins
1 cup pecans, chopped

Preheat oven to 325 degrees. Grease and flour a 9-inch square pan.

In large bowl, beat eggs. Add oil and sugar. Mix well. Stir in flour, baking powder, baking soda, salt, cinnamon, and nutmeg. Stir in bourbon. Add carrots, raisins, and pecans. Mix well.

Pour into pan. Bake for 40 minutes. Cool in pan. Spread with glaze.

Bourbon Glaze:
1 cup confectioners' sugar
2 Tablespoons hot water
1 Tablespoon bourbon

Blend together and spread on cooled cake.

BRANDIED STUFFED DATES

1 pound pitted dates
1 cup brandy
1 cup pecan halves
sugar, if desired

Soak dates in brandy, turning occasionally, until most of the brandy is absorbed, about 24 hours. Place a pecan half in each date; press to close. Roll in sugar. Store in airtight container in refrigerator.

CREME DE MENTHE BARS

1 cup sugar
½ cup butter, softened
4 eggs, slightly beaten
1 cup flour
½ tsp salt
1 tsp vanilla
1 (16 oz) can Hershey's chocolate

Preheat oven to 350 degrees.
In large bowl, cream together sugar and butter. Mix in eggs, vanilla, salt and chocolate. Add flour. Mix well. Pour into ungreased 9 x 13 pan. Bake for 30 minutes. Cool.

Topping:
2 cups confectioners' sugar
3 Tablespoons green creme de Menthe
½ cup butter, softened
6 oz. chocolate chips
6 Tablespoons butter

Cream sugar, ½ cup butter, and creme de Menthe. Spread over cooled bars. Melt chocolate chips and 6 Tablespoons butter together. Cool slightly and drizzle over top. Chill bars 10 minutes. Cut into small squares.

IRISH CREAM CHOCOLATE CHIP COOKIES

1 stick butter, softened
½ cup granulated sugar
½ cup brown sugar
1 egg
½ cup Irish Cream
2 1/4 cup flour
½ tsp baking soda
½ tsp salt
6 oz. package semi sweet chocolate chips
½ cup chopped pecan OR walnuts
3/4 cup coconut (optional)

Preheat oven to 375 degrees.

In large mixing bowl, cream butter, sugars and egg until fluffy. Add vanilla and Irish Cream. In separate bowl, mix flour, soda, and salt. Blend dry mixture into creamed mixture. Add chips, nuts, and coconut. Drop heaping teaspoon size cookies onto ungreased baking sheets. Bake for 8-10 minutes. Cool slightly before removing from sheet to cooling rack.

BISCOTTI

1 cup flour
1 tsp baking soda
1 cup unprocessed wheat bran
½ cup unsalted butter, softened
1 cup sugar
1 egg
1 Tablespoon dark rum
1 tsp vanilla

Preheat oven to 350 degrees. Grease large cookie sheets.

In mixing bowl, sift together flour and baking soda. Stir in the bran and set aside.

In large mixing bowl, combine butter and sugar. With mixer, on medium speed, beat until fluffy, light and pale in color; about 5 minutes. Continue beating while adding the egg. Beat in the rum and vanilla. Reduce the speed to low and add the flour mixture, 1/3 at a time, beating well after each addition until thoroughly incorporated.

Spoon dough onto prepared sheet to form 10 - 11 inch strip. Using moistened fingertips, shape dough into a neat 11 x 2 ½ inch log.

Bake until log just begins to brown and feels firm to touch, about 20 minutes. Cool cookie log on sheet 15 minutes. Maintain oven temperature.

Transfer cookie log to cutting board. Using serrated knife, cut crosswise into 1/3-inch-wide slices. Arrange slices on same baking sheet. Bake 10 minutes. Turn slices over. Bake until beginning to color, about 8 minutes longer. Cool cookies completely on baking sheet. (Cookies will become very crisp.)

Just right for dipping into dessert wine or cappuccino.

Can be prepared 1 week ahead. Store in airtight container at room temperature. Makes about 2 dozen

KOURABIEDES WITH CINNAMON

Greek Cookies

1 cup butter, softened
½ cup confectioners' sugar, plus additional sugar for sprinkling
1 egg yolks
1 Tablespoons cinnamon
½ tsp baking powder
2 1/4 cups flour
2 Tablespoons brandy
½ tsp vanilla
1/3 cup almonds, toasted, skins on, coarsely ground

In mixing bowl, with electric mixer, beat butter until light and fluffy. Slowly add confectioners' sugar. Add egg yolk, brandy and vanilla. Mix well. Mix cinnamon and baking powder with 1 cup flour. Slowly add flour mixture plus brandy to the butter mixture, beating well. Add more flour, working it in by hand to form a soft dough. Add almonds to the dough. Wrap in plastic wrap and refrigerate dough for 1 hour.

Preheat oven to 325 degrees.

Shape dough into 1-inch balls and make small "c" shapes about ½ inch thick and place on a cookie sheet. Bake for 20 - 25 minutes or until a light sand color. Sprinkle with confectioners' sugar while still warm. Makes 3 ½ dozen.

BRANDIED CARAMEL FLAN

3/4 cup sugar
1 can (14oz) evaporated milk
1/4 cup water
2 cups heavy cream
6 eggs
½ cup sugar
½ tsp salt
2 tsp vanilla
1/4 cup brandy

To prepare the caramelized sugar coating, spread the 3/4 cup sugar evenly in the bottom of a heavy saucepan and place over medium-low heat. Without stirring, watch the sugar closely as it begins to liquify at the edges. It may take several minutes. Shake and swirl occasionally to distribute sugar, but do not stir. It will slowly turn first to a yellowish and then golden syrup and finally into a brown caramel sauce. Immediately remove the saucepan from the heat or it will turn too dark and taste bitter.

Quickly pour caramel into a 1 ½ qt casserole dish or 12 custard cups and tilt to cover the bottom and sides evenly. Set aside.

Preheat oven to 350 degrees. Boil some water.

In saucepan, heat milk, water and cream just until bubbles form around edges. Set aside to cool. In large mixing bowl, beat eggs slightly. Add ½ cup sugar, salt and vanilla. Gradually add milk mixture and brandy.

Pour into baking dish(s). Place dishes, not touching each other, in a large, deep pan. Pull out oven rack to place pan on rack. Pour boiling water into the pan to create a water bath about 1 inch deep. Bake 45-60 minutes or until knife comes out clean. Remove water bath from oven and then carefully remove the custards from the water bath and set aside to cool completely. Refrigerate 4 hours. Run spatula around edge to loosen. Invert onto serving plate.

SWEET PASTRY SQUARES

1 egg yolk
½ cup flour
½ cup butter, softened
2 Tablespoons sugar
2 Tablespoons white wine

jam or fruit spread
1 egg, beaten with 1 Tablespoon water
coarse sugar
sliced almonds

In large bowl, combine egg yolk, flour, butter, sugar, and wine. Knead into a smooth dough and let rest, covered, for ½ hour.

Preheat oven to 400 degrees.

Roll out dough to about 1/4 inch thickness and cut into 3 inch squares. Place a heaping teaspoon of the fruit/jam in the center of each square. Fold the four corners of the square toward the center, being sure that the filling is still visible. Brush cookies with beaten egg. Sprinkle with course sugar and almonds. Bake until golden brown; about 10 minutes.

IRISH CREAM SUGAR COOKIES

2 sticks butter, softened
1 ½ cups sugar
1 tsp vanilla
1 egg + 1 yolk, slightly beaten
½ cup Irish cream liqueur
4 cups flour
½ tsp salt
1 Tablespoon baking powder

In large bowl, cream together butter and sugar until fluffy. Beat in egg and vanilla. Add Irish cream.

Sift together flour, salt and baking powder. Stir into butter mixture. Form into a ball and flatten. Wrap well with plastic wrap and refrigerate 2 hours or more.

Preheat oven to 350 degrees.

On floured work surface, roll dough to 1/4 inch thickness. Cut into shapes and place onto baking sheets. Bake until golden brown around the edges, 6-8 minutes. Cool on a wire rack.

KAHLUA FLAN

3/4 cup sugar
4 eggs
1 (14 oz) can sweetened condensed milk
1 (12 oz) can evaporated milk
2 Tablespoons Kahlua
chocolate shavings for garnish

Preheat oven to 350 degrees.

In small saucepan, cook, without stirring, the sugar over medium heat until it starts to melt. Lower the heat and cook until caramelized to a golden brown. Swirl pan to melt evenly.

Pour into 9-inch cake pan. Swirl to evenly coat the bottom. Let cool.

In large bowl, whisk the eggs. Add the milks and Kahlua. Blend. Place the cake pan into a larger roasting pan. Pour the milk mixture into the cake pan. Open the oven and pull out the rack. Place the roasting pan on the rack. Pour hot water into the roasting pan to come halfway up the sides of the cake pan. Carefully slide the rack in and close the door. Bake until set and just firm in the center, but still jiggles slightly, 50 - 60 minutes. Remove pan from water bath. Let cool on a wire rack. Refrigerate at least 2 hours.

To serve, run a thin sharp knife around the rim of the flan. Place a platter on to of the flan and gently flip over so the plate is on the bottom. Lift away the cake pan. Garnish with chocolate shavings. Cut into wedges and serve immediately.

Serves 6 - 8

RUM RAISIN OATMEAL COOKIES

2 sticks of butter, softened

1 cup brown sugar, packed

½ cup sugar

2 eggs, beaten

1 tsp vanilla

1 Tablespoon rum

1 ½ cup flour

1 tsp baking soda

1 tsp cinnamon

½ tsp salt

3 cups oats

1 cups raisins, soaked overnight in rum

Preheat oven to 35 degrees.

In large mixing bowl, beat together butter and sugars until creamy. Add eggs, vanilla and rum. Beat well. Sift together flour baking soda, cinnamon, and salt. Add to mixture. Mix well. Stir in oats and then raisins.

Drop by heaping Tablespoons onto an ungreased cookie sheet, 2 inches apart. Bake 10-12 minutes or until golden brown. Cool 1 minute on cookie sheet before removing to wire rack to cool completely.

BLACK FOREST RUGALACH

Filling:

1 cup dried cherries

1/3 cup kirsch

2/3 cup sugar

6 oz semi-sweet chocolate, broken

2 Tablespoons unsweetened cocoa powder

1 tsp ground cinnamon

1 cup walnuts

Dough:

8 oz cream cheese, softened

2 sticks butter, softened

2 cups flour

pinch salt

For Assembly:

1 egg

1 tsp water

Filling: In a small bowl, combine the dried cherries and kirsch. Cover and let stand at least 4 hours, stirring occasionally.

Dough: Meanwhile, in a large bowl, with electric mixer on high speed, blend the cream cheese and butter until fluffy and light. Gradually beat in the flour and salt. The dough will be very soft. Divide and flatten the dough into 4 disks. Wrap each in plastic wrap and refrigerate until firm enough to handle; at least 1 hour.

Back to filling: Drain cherries and set aside. In food processor, place the sugar, chocolate, cocoa and cinnamon; cover and pulse chop until the chocolate forms pea-sized pieces. Add the walnuts and cherries; continue to pulse chop until both are coarsely chopped.

Back to dough: On lightly floured surface, roll out dough, one disk at a time, to form an 8-inch circle. In a small bowl, beat together the egg and water. Brush the dough with the egg glaze. Sprinkle 1/4 of the filling over the top, pressing lightly to adhere the filling to the dough. Cut the circle into 12 wedges with a shape knife.

Roll up each wedge, from the wide end, to form a crescent. Tuck in any filling that falls out. Place the crescents, point side down, 1 inch apart on ungreased cookie sheet. Brush with additional egg glaze.

Bake for 30 - 35 minutes, or until golden. Cool on the cookie sheets for about 2 minutes. Gently loosen them with a metal spatula and transfer to wire racks to cool completely. Store in airtight containers.

STRAWBERRY AND IRISH CREAM FOOL

1 pint strawberries, washed and hulled, reserve 6 small berries for garnish
2 cups heavy whipping cream
½ cup Irish cream
confectioners' sugar for dusting

Chill 6 stem glasses while preparing fruit. In food processor or blender, puree strawberries until smooth. In a bowl, with an electric mixer, whip cream, on high, until stiff. Add half the strawberry puree and the Irish cream to the whip cream and blend until smooth. Divide the mixture into the bottom quarter of each glass. Spoon over some of the fruit puree, and continue to alternate layers of cream with fruit. Slice the reserved berries to top each glass and sprinkle with confectioners' sugar.

Serves 6

RUM RAISIN RING CAKE

1 (20 oz) can crushed pineapple in juice
1 ½ cup sugar
1 stick of butter, softened
3 eggs, beaten
1 tsp vanilla
2 ½ cups flour
1 tsp baking powder
1 tsp baking soda
1 tsp allspice
½ tsp salt
½ cup rum
1 cup raisins
1 cup chopped walnuts
Rum Glaze

Preheat oven to 350 degrees. Grease a 10-inch Bundt pan.

Into a large measuring cup, drain pineapple, reserving juice - 1/4 cup for cake and 3 Tablespoons for glaze.

In large bowl, cream sugar and butter. Beat in eggs and vanilla. Sift together flour, baking powder, soda, allspice and salt. Alternating flour mixture and 1/4 cup pineapple juice and the rum, mix into butter mixture. Stir in drained pineapple, raisins, and nuts.

Bake 55-60 minutes or until tester comes out clean. Invert on wire rack. Cool completely before glazing.

Glaze:
2 Tablespoons rum
2 Tablespoons pineapple juice
2 Tablespoons butter, softened
2 cups confectioners' sugar
Beat until blended. Glaze cake.

PINA COLADA WEDGES

1 (8 oz) package cream cheese, softened
1/3 cup sugar
2 Tablespoons rum
3 ½ cups cool whip, thawed, divided
1 (8 1/4 oz) can crushed pineapple, undrained
2 2/3 cups (7 oz) coconut flakes, divided
small can sliced pineapple
maraschino cherries

Beat cream cheese with sugar and rum until smooth. Fold in 2 cups of whipped topping, pineapple, and 2 cups of coconut. Spread in 8 inch round layer pan lined with plastic wrap. Invert pan onto serving plate; remove pan and plastic wrap. Spread with remaining whipped topping and sprinkle with the remaining coconut. Freeze until firm, about 2 hours. Cut into wedges. Garnish with pineapple and cherries.

CRANBERRY RUM COFFEECAKE

1 cup Craisins
1 stick butter
1 cup warm tap water
1/4 cup rum
1/4 cup cold water

1 ½ cups flour
1 cup granulated sugar
1 tsp baking soda
½ tsp salt
1 tsp cinnamon
1/4 tsp ginger
1/4 tsp nutmeg
3/4 cup chopped nuts

2 Tablespoons butter, melted
confectioners sugar

In medium saucepan, combine Craisins, butter and 1 cup of water. Bring to a boil. Reduce heat to low and simmer for 5 minutes. Remove from heat and allow to cool to room temperature. Stir in rum and cold water.

Preheat oven to 350 degrees. Grease and flour 8-inch square baking pan.

In medium bowl, combine flour, granulated sugar, baking soda, salt, cinnamon, ginger, and nutmeg. Set aside. In another bowl, with electric mixer, beat egg until light and fluffy. Stir in Craisin mixture. Gradually stir in the dry ingredient mixture. Stir just until mixed. Some lumps may remain. Fold in chopped nuts.

Pour into baking dish. Bake for 35-40 minutes or until tester comes out nearly clean. Remove from oven. Brush top with melted butter and dust lightly with confectioners' sugar while still warm.

FANCY FROSTING

Mocha:

1 (16oz) can milk chocolate frosting
2 Tablespoons coffee liqueur
Mix and spread.

Cherry:

1 (16oz) can vanilla frosting
2 Tablespoons kirsch
Mix and spread.

Vanilla:

1 (16oz) can vanilla frosting
2 Tablespoons amaretto
Mix and spread.

Orange:

1 (16oz) can vanilla frosting
2 Tablespoons orange liqueur
Mix and spread.

CHERRY CORDIAL PIE

1 ½ cups chocolate wafer cookies, crushed
1/4 cup butter, melted

½ cup milk
32 large marshmallows
½ cup Kirsch
1 ½ cups chilled heavy whipping cream
1 - 2 drops red food color (optional)
1 - 2 oz semi-sweet chocolate, grated (optional)

For cookie crumb crust:
Preheat oven to 350 degrees.
Mix crumbs and butter. Press mixture firmly against bottom and sides of 9-inch pie plate. Bake 10 minutes. Cool.

For Filling:
In microwave bowl, combine Kirsch, milk, and marshmallows. Microwave on high for 1 minute. Stir until fully melted. In mixing bowl, beat whipping cream until stiff. Add food color, if desired. Fold whipping cream into marshmallow mixture. Pour into crust. Sprinkle with grated semi-sweet chocolate, if desired. Refrigerate until set, about 4 hours.

ALEXANDER PIE

1 ½ cups chocolate wafer cookies, crushed
1/4 cup butter, melted

½ cup milk
32 large marshmallows
1/4 cup creme de cacao
3 Tablespoons brandy
1 ½ cups chilled heavy whipping cream
1 - 2 oz semi-sweet chocolate, grated (optional)

For cookie crumb crust:
Preheat oven to 350 degrees.
Mix crumbs and butter. Press mixture firmly against bottom and sides of 9-inch pie plate. Bake 10 minutes. Cool.

For Filling:
In microwave bowl, combine milk and marshmallows. Microwave on high for 1 minute. Stir until fully melted. Add creme de cacao and brandy. Stir. In mixing bowl, beat whipping cream until stiff. Fold whipping cream into marshmallow mixture. Pour into crust. Sprinkle with grated semi-sweet chocolate, if desired. Refrigerate until set, about 4 hours.

CINNAMON-RAISIN BISCOTTI

1 large egg
½ cup sugar
1 Tablespoon brandy
1 tsp vanilla
3/4 cup plus 2 Tablespoons all-purpose flour
3/4 tsp baking powder
3/4 tsp ground cinnamon
1/4 tsp salt
1/3 cup raisins
1/3 cup whole almonds, toasted

Preheat over to 375 degrees. Lightly grease heavy large baking sheet.

Using hand-held electric mixer, beat egg and sugar in medium bowl until very thick and fluffy, about 2 minutes. Beat in brandy and vanilla. Sift together, flour baking powder, cinnamon and salt. Add to egg mixture and blend well. Mix in raisins and almonds.

Spoon dough onto prepared sheet to form 10 - 11 inch strip. Using moistened fingertips, shape dough into a neat 11 x 2 ½ inch log.

Bake until log just begins to brown and feels firm to touch, about 20 minutes. Cool cookie log on sheet 15 minutes. Maintain oven temperature.

Transfer cookie log to cutting board. Using serrated knife, cut crosswise into 1/3-inch-wide slices. Arrange slices on same baking sheet. Bake 10 minutes. Turn slices over. Bake until beginning to color, about 8 minuets longer. Cool cookies completely on baking sheet. (Cookies will become very crisp.)

Can be prepared 1 week ahead. Store in airtight container at room temperature. Makes about 2 dozen

CRANBERRY ICE CREAM PIE

2 chocolate flavored crumb pie shells
1 quart vanilla ice cream, softened
1(16oz) can whole cranberry sauce
2 Tablespoons Grand Marnier
1 (8oz) carton frozen whipped dessert topping, thawed
2 Tablespoons toasted slice almonds
Additional whole cranberry sauce thinned with Grand Marnier

Place pie shells in freezer while preparing filling. In large bowl, mix ice cream, cranberry sauce, and Grand Marnier with large spoon, until combined. Spoon filling into chilled pie shells. Freeze until firm, at least 4 hours. Spread whipped toping and sprinkle with almonds. Cover. Return to freezer until serving time. For easier cutting, remover from freezer 5-10 minutes before serving. To serve, spoon cranberry sauce over each serving. Makes 2 pies.

HAZELNUT POACHED PEARS

1 3/4 cups brown sugar, packed
1 ½ cups water
1/3 cup Frangelico
5 small firm, but ripe, pears, peeled, cored, halved lengthwise

In heavy large, wide, saucepan, combine sugar, water and Frangelico. Stir over medium heat until sugar dissolves. Bring to boil. Add pears. Cover and simmer until pears are fork tender, turning occasionally, about 12 minutes. Using slotted spoon, transfer pears to medium bowl. Boil cooking liquid in pan until syrupy and reduced to about 3/4 cup (about 5 minutes).

Pour syrup over pears and cool. Cover and chill.

Serves 10

BAKED BANANAS IN LEMON-RUM SAUCE

4 very ripe bananas

Sauce:
1 Tablespoon grated lemon rind
2 Tablespoons lemon juice
2 Tablespoons sugar
3 Tablespoons orange marmalade
1/4 cup water
2 Tablespoons dark rum

Preheat oven to 400 degrees. Trim about ½ inch off ends of bananas. Cut an end-to-end slit through the skin of each banana. Place on cookie sheet and bake for 15 minutes. (Skin will turn black).

In saucepan, mix together the remaining ingredients. Bring to a boil, stirring to prevent sticking. Boil 1 minute. Remove from heat.

When bananas are cool enough to handle, remove the skin and place them in a serving dish. Pour sauce over bananas and coat all sides. Serve.
4 servings

AMARETTO APPLES

2 medium Golden Delicious apples, peeled, cored, diced
1 ½ Tablespoon butter
2 Tablespoons sugar
2 Tablespoons raisins
2 Tablespoons Amaretto
2 Tablespoons sliced almonds, toasted
whipped cream

In skillet over medium-high heat, melt butter. Add apples. Sprinkle with sugar and saute until tender, about 6 minutes. Stir in raisins. Add Amaretto and cook until liquid reduces to glaze, about 1 minute. Divide into 2 dessert dishes. Garnish with almonds and whipped cream. Serve immediately.

BLACK BOTTOM PIE

½ (15oz) packaged refrigerated pie crusts
1 (3oz) package vanilla pudding mix
2 cups milk
1 cup semisweet chocolate chips
1 Tablespoon rum
1 cup whipping cream, whipped

Fit pie crust into a 9-inch pie-plate; fold edges under, and crimp. Bake according to package directions.

In small saucepan, combine pudding mix and milk; cook per package instructions for pie filling. Remove ½ cup hot pudding; add chocolate chips, stirring until smooth. Spoon into pie crust. Stir rum into remaining pudding. Spoon evenly over chocolate mixture. Chill 2 hours. Serve with whipped cream.

KAHLUA & CREAM FUDGE

1 (12 oz) package semi-sweet chocolate chips
1 (12 oz) package white chocolate chips
1 (14 oz) can fat-free sweetened condensed milk, divided
5 Tablespoons Kahlua, divided
salt

Line a 8 inch or 9 inch square pan with aluminum foil; set aside.

In microwave bowl, combine semi-sweet chocolate, 7 Tablespoons milk, 3 Tablespoons Kahlua, and a dash of salt. Microwave on high for 1 minute. Stir to melt and mix. Spread in pan.

In clean bowl, combine white chocolate, 1/2 cup milk and 2 Tablespoons Kahlua. Microwave on high for one minute. Stir. Microwave additional 20 seconds, if needed to complete melting. Stir. Spread over first layer of chocolate. Chill at least 2 hours.

Turn upside-down to remove from pan. Remove foil. Cut into bite-size pieces. Store covered.

KAHLUA BANANA COFFEECAKE

1 cup butter, softened
1 ½ cups sugar
3 ½ cups flour, sifted
1 cup mashed ripe bananas
½ cup Kahlua
4 eggs, slightly beaten
1/4 cup milk
1 Tablespoon baking powder
1 tsp baking soda
1 tsp salt
3/4 cup flaked coconut
3/4 cup chopped walnuts
confectioners' sugar for dusting

Preheat oven to 350 degrees. Spray Bundt pan with non-stick cooking spray.

In large mixing bowl, cream butter and sugar until fluffy. Beat in eggs. Mix in flour, ½ cup at a time. Mix in baking powder, baking soda, and salt. Mix in milk, Kahlua, and bananas. Stir in coconut and walnuts. Turn into prepared pan. Bake 45 - 50 minutes, or until golden brown. Remove from oven and let stand 10 minutes. Invert onto rack to cool and remove from pan. When fully cool, dust with confectioners' sugar.

BLACK FOREST CAKE

2 cups flour, sifted

2 cups sugar

3/4 cup cocoa

1 1/4 tsp baking powder

1/4 tsp baking soda

3/4 tsp salt

½ cup butter, softened

½ cup sour cream, divided

½ cup milk

1/3 cup kirsch

2 eggs + 2 egg yolks

4 cups whipping cream

1/3 cup confectioners' sugar

2 Tablespoons kirsch

2 (21 oz) cans cherry pie filling

Preheat oven to 350 degrees. Grease two 9-inch round cake pans; line bottoms with wax paper. Grease and flour wax paper and sides of pans.

In large bowl, combine flour, sugar, cocoa, baking powder, soda, and salt. Add butter and 1/4 cup sour cream; beat at low speed with electric mixer just until dry ingredients are moistened, about 30 seconds. Add remaining 1/4 cup sour cream, milk, and 1/3 cup kirsch. Beat at medium speed 1 ½ minutes. Add eggs and egg yolks, one at a time, beating mixture after each addition.

Pour batter into pans. Bake for 30-35 minutes or until tester comes out clean. Cool in pans on wire racks for 10 minutes; remove from pans. Peel off wax paper, and cool cake layers on wire racks. Split cake layers in half horizontally to make 4 layers.

In food processor, break 1 cake layer into pieces and pulse 5 - 6 times or until cake resembles fine crumbs. Set aside. Beat whipping cream until foamy; gradually add confectioners' sugar, beating until soft peaks form. Add 2 Tablespoons kirsch, beating until stiff peaks form. Reserve 1 ½ cups whipped cream mixture for garnish.

Place 1 layer on cake plate; spread with 1 cup whipped cream mixture and top with 1 cup pie filling. Repeat with each layer. Frost with whipped cream mixture. Pat cake crumbs around sides of cake. Spoon 1 cup of pie filling in center of cake top. Dollop reserved 1 ½ cups whipped cream mixture around top edges of cake.

Cover and chill 8 hours.

CHOCOLATE MINT CAKE

½ cup butter, softened
4 oz cream cheese, softened
2 cups sugar
2 eggs
2 tsp vanilla
2 cups flour
3/4 cup cocoa
1 ½ tsp baking soda
½ tsp salt
3/4 cup boiling water
1/4 cup creme de menthe

Preheat oven to 350 degrees. Grease and flour two 9-inch round cake pans or one 9 x 13 pan.

In large bowl, cream butter, cream cheese, and sugar until fluffy. Beat in eggs and vanilla. In medium bowl, sift together flour, cocoa, baking soda, and salt. Add dry ingredients to creamed mixture; beat until smooth. Add water and creme de menthe; beat until smooth. Pour batter into pans. Bake 25-30 minutes or until tester comes out clean. Cool in pans 10 minutes, if using rounds. Remove from round pans and cool completely on wire rack. Cool 9 x 13 cake before frosting.

Frosting:
3 ½ cups confectioners' sugar, sifted
3 Tablespoons creme de menthe
½ cup butter, softened
1 Tablespoon vanilla
green food color - optional

Beat all ingredients together until smooth. If frosting is too thin, thicken with additional sugar. If using rounds, frost between layers, sides and top of cake. Frost top of 9 x 13.

HARVEY WALLBANGER CAKE

1 package orange cake mix
1 package instant vanilla pudding
½ cup orange juice
½ cup Galliano liqueur
4 eggs, beaten
½ cup vegetable oil
2 Tablespoons vodka

Preheat oven to 350 degrees. Grease and flour Bundt pan or angle food cake pan.

Place all ingredients into a large mixing bowl; beat 5 minutes or until well blended. Pour into pan. Bake about 45 minutes or until tester comes out clean. Remove from oven. Invert on wire rack. Cool cake for 10 minutes. (While cake is baking, prepare glaze for topping.)

Glaze:
1 3/4 cups confectioners' sugar
3 tsp orange juice
2 tsp Galliano liqueur
1 tsp vodka

Mix. Pour over warm cake.

TENNESSE WHISKEY FRUIT CAKE

1 cup butter, softened
2 cups brown sugar
4 eggs, beaten
3 cups flour
1 tsp baking soda
½ tsp salt
1 ½ cups Tennessee whiskey, divided
½ cup orange juice
3 cups pecan pieces
2 cups dried apricots, chopped
2 cups golden raisins
2 cups dates, chopped

cheesecloth
whiskey

Preheat oven to 325 degrees. Grease three 9 x5 inch loaf pans. Line pan bottoms with wax paper.

In large bowl, with electric mixer, cream together butter and brown sugar until light and fluffy. Add eggs; beat well. In medium bowl, sift together flour, baking soda and salt. Add flour mixture to butter mixture, alternately with ½ cup whiskey and orange juice. Beat on low speed just until blended. Stir in fruits and nuts. Spoon into pans. Bake about 1 hour and 15 minutes, or until tester comes out clean. Cool in pans on wire rack. Remove from pans to cool completely; remove wax paper.
Wrap each loaf in whiskey soaked cheesecloth. Wrap tightly in plastic wrap, then aluminum foil. Store in refrigerator for two weeks before serving. Serve thinly sliced.

BRANDY SNAPS

1 stick butter
3 Tablespoons molasses
½ cup flour
½ cup sugar
1 Tablespoon ground ginger
1/4 tsp salt
2 Tablespoons brandy

Preheat oven to 350 degrees. Grease large cookie sheet.

In small saucepan, over medium heat, combine butter and molasses. Cook until butter melts. Remove from heat. Stir in flour, sugar, ginger, and salt. Stir in brandy until blended. Keep warm over very low heat.

Drop 1 teaspoon of mixture onto cookie sheet, spread into 4-inch round. Repeat to make 3 more rounds, about 2 inches apart.

Bake for 5 minutes, until golden brown. Remove cookie sheet from oven. Allow cookies to cool only until set. With pancake turner, quickly turn cookies over, so lacy texture will be on outside of cookie.

Roll cookies into cylinders around the handle of a wooden spoon. Remove from handle to wire rack to cool completely. (If cookies become too hard to roll, return to oven briefly to soften.

Store in tightly covered container. Makes about 3 dozen fragile cookies.

MUD CAKE

7 oz unsweetened chocolate
3/4 cup butter
1 ½ cups strong coffee
1/4 cup bourbon
2 eggs
1 tsp vanilla
2 cups flour
1 ½ cups sugar
1 tsp baking soda
1/4 tsp salt

Preheat the oven to 325 degrees. Grease and lightly flour two 9 x 5 inch loaf pans.

In a heavy-bottomed saucepan, combine chocolate, butter, and coffee. Place over low heat and stir almost constantly until the chocolate melts, then stir vigorously to blend and smooth the mixture completely. Set aside to cool for about 10 minutes, then beat in the bourbon, eggs, and vanilla. Sift together the flour, sugar, baking soda, and salt. Add the dry mix to the chocolate mixture and beat with a wooden spoon to blend and smooth.

Divide the batter evenly between the two prepared pans. Bake for 45-55 minutes, or until tester comes out clean. Remove from the oven and cool for about 15 minutes. Turn cakes out onto cooling racks.

Suggested service: with whipped cream or raspberry sauce

AMARETTO BUTTER COOKIES

2 sticks of butter, softened
1 cup sugar
1/4 tsp salt
1 egg, separated
1 ½ Tablespoons Amaretto
2 tsp grated orange rind
2 cups flour
3/4 cup sliced almonds

Preheat oven to 300 degrees.

Combine the butter and sugar in a mixing bowl and beat until smooth. Add the salt, egg yolk, Amaretto, and orange rind. Beat until blended. Stir in the flour and blend thoroughly. Spread and pat the dough evenly over the bottom of an ungreased 10 x 15-inch jelly-roll pan.

Beat the egg white just until foamy, spread it evenly over the dough, then sprinkle the almonds over all. Bake for about 45 minutes, or until lightly golden. Remove from the oven and cut into about 2-inch squares while still warm.

SPARKLING CHAMPAGNE GELATIN

1 ½ cups boiling water
2 pkg (4-serving size) Sparkling White Grape or Lemon Flavor gelatin
1 cup cold champagne
1 cup cold ginger ale
1 cup sliced strawberries

Stir boiling water into gelatin in large bowl at least 2 minutes until completely dissolved. Refrigerate 15 minutes. Gently stir in cold champagne and ginger ale. Refrigerate about 1 hour or until slightly thickened (spoon drawn through leaves definite impression).

Measure 1 cup thickened gelatin into medium bowl; set aside. Stir strawberries into remaining gelatin. Spoon into champagne glasses or dessert dishes.

Beat reserved gelatin with electric mixer on high speed until fluffy and about doubled in volume. Spoon over clear gelatin in glasses. Refrigerate 2 hours or until firm.

APPLE WINE PIE

1/3 cup raisins

½ cup brown sugar

2 Tablespoon butter

½ tsp cinnamon

1/4 cup red wine

7 cups sliced apple (Pippins or Golden Delicious)

2 Tablespoons sugar

2 pie crusts (follow package directions)

Preheat oven to 425 degrees.

In a small saucepan, combine raisins, brown sugar, butter, cinnamon, and wine. Bring to a boil, stirring occasionally. Let simmer for 1 minute. Remove from heat. Let cool while preparing crust. Stir in sliced apples.

Place one pie crust in bottom of pie pan and gently shape to pan. Pour in apple mixture. Top with crust. Flute edge. Cut slits in top. Bake 30 minutes. Reduce heat to 350 degrees and bake additional 20-30 minutes until juices bubble up around the edges and through the vents and the crust is browned. A sharp knife inserted through one of the vents should pierce the apples easily. If the crust browns too quickly, cover the edges loosely with 2-inch strips of foil and continue baking.

Sauces,
Toppings & Frostings

Let him kiss me with the kisses of his mouth -
for your love is more delightful than wine.

Song of Songs 1:2

WHISKEY GLAZE

3/4 cup sugar
1 stick butter
½ cup whiskey

In saucepan, combine all ingredients. Heat, over medium heat, until sugar dissolves, stirring constantly.

RAISIN BEER SAUCE

1/4 cup brown sugar, packed
1 ½ Tablespoons cornstarch
1/8 tsp salt
1 cup beer, room temperature
1/4 cup raisins, cut in half
1/4 tsp ground cloves
1 tsp ground cinnamon
1 Tablespoon butter

In saucepan, combine brown sugar, cornstarch, cloves, cinnamon and salt. Stir in beer and raisins. Bring to a boil. Reduce heat and simmer 10 minutes. Stir in butter.
Makes about 1 ½ cups

CRANBERRY HONEY GLAZE

4 Tablespoons rum
1/4 cup honey
1 cup jellied cranberry sauce

In small saucepan, combine all ingredients. Cook over medium heat, jut unitl sauce is smooth, whisking often. Makes about 1 cup.

AMARETTO CARAMEL SAUCE

1 cup firmly packed brown sugar
1 cup whipping cream
1/4 cup light corn syrup
2 Tablespoons butter
2 Tablespoons amaretto

In medium saucepan, combine all ingredients except amaretto. Bring to a boil, stirring occasionally. Reduce heat; boil gently 8-10 minutes or until slightly thickened. Remove from heat; stir in amaretto. Serve warm over ice cream or cake.

BRANDIED BUTTERSCOTCH SAUCE

3 cups brown sugar, packed
1 cup light corn syrup
½ cup butter
½ cup whipping cream
1 Tablespoon brandy

Heat brown sugar, corn syrup and butter to boiling over medium heat, stirring constantly. Remove from heat; stir in whipping cream and brandy. Cool. Pour into jars; cover tightly. Refrigerate no longer than 3 months. Serve warm, over vanilla ice cream.

Makes 3 ½ cups sauce

WHITE CHOCOLATE RUM SAUCE

6 oz white chocolate, chopped
1/3 cup rum

In microwave bowl, combine and melt for 1 minute on high. Stir until smooth. Serve at room temperature or slightly warm.

BRANDY PEACH SAUCE

2 fresh ripe peaches, peeled and sliced
1 Tablespoon butter
2 Tablespoons sugar
2 Tablespoons brandy
1/4 cup water
1 tsp cornstarch

In saucepan, melt butter. Add peaches and sugar. Cook over medium heat, stirring, for a few minutes. Add brandy and water and boil for 5 minutes. Dissolve cornstarch in a little cold water. Add to peaches, bring to a boil, stirring constantly. Remove from heat.

RASPBERRY-RUM SAUCE

½ cup seedless raspberry preserves
1 Tablespoon dark rum
1 Tablespoon water

Mix and serve.

BRANDY BUTTER SAUCE

2/3 cup sugar
2 Tablespoons cornstarch
1/8 tsp salt
1 1/4 cups water
3 Tablespoons butter
1/4 cup brandy

In heavy-bottomed saucepan, combine the sugar, cornstarch and salt. Mix well. Slowly add the water, stirring constantly, until the mixture is smooth. Cook, over medium-low heat, stirring constantly, until the sauce thickens and becomes translucent. Remove from the heat and stir in the butter. Then, stir in the brandy. Refrigerate left overs. Gently reheat when needed.

RASPBERRY GRAND MARNIER SAUCE

1 ½ cups orange juice
1 cup Melba sauce
1 cup raspberries (fresh or frozen)
½ cup Grand Marnier

In saucepan, combine all ingredients. Bring to a boil, over medium heat, stirring constantly. Boil 1 minute. Remove from heat. Cool.

BOURBON FILLING

(for white or yellow layer cake)

4 egg yolks

½ cup sugar
1/8 tsp salt
½ cup bourbon
4 Tablespoons butter, melted
½ cup raisins
½ cup shredded coconut

½ cup chopped walnuts

In a heavy-bottomed saucepan, combine the egg yolks, sugar, and salt. Beat for a few minutes, until the mixture is pale and thick. Add the bourbon and melted butter and blend well. Cook over medium-low heat, stirring slowly but constantly, until it feels very hot to your finger; it will thicken just slightly, and you will see wisps of steam rising, but it should not boil. Remove from the heat and add the raisins, coconut, and walnuts. Blend well. Cool before using. Refrigerate for storage. Makes enough to fill a 9-inch three-layer cake.

STRAWBERRY CHAMPAGNE SAUCE

5 cups strawberries
3/4 cup Champagne or sparkling white wine
1/4 cup sugar

In a blender container combine all ingredients. Cover and blend until smooth. (Or, in food processor, work with half at a time.) Cover and chill for several hours or overnight. Makes 4 cups.

BLUEBERRY SAUCE

1/4 cup apricot preserves
2 Tablespoons cognac
1 cup fresh blueberries

Mix the preserves and cognac together in small bowl, adding 1 Tablespoon water, if needed, to thin the preserves to the consistency of a sauce. Stir in the blueberries.

BLACK CURRANT SAUCE

10 oz strawberries, hulled
5 oz black currant preserves (with berries)
2 Tablespoons creme de Cassis

Puree strawberries and preserves together. Add creme de Cassis. Stir and serve.

IRISH CREAM FROSTING

1 stick butter, softened
2 1/4 cups confectioners' sugar
1/4 cup Irish creme liqueur

In large bowl, with electric mixer, cream the butter until smooth. Gradually beat in the confectioners' sugar. Beat in Irish cream until frosting is light and fluffy.

PEPPERMINT BUTTERCREAM FROSTING

1 stick butter, softened
½ cup finely crushed peppermint candy (about 7 sticks)
3 cups confectioners' sugar, sifted
2 - 3 Tablespoons milk
1 - 2 Tablespoons peppermint schnapps

In large mixing bowl, beat butter on low speed until fluffy, about 30 seconds. Stop mixer. Add peppermint candy, sugar, 2 Tablespoons milk and 1 Tablespoon peppermint schnapps. Blend with the mixer on low until the sugar is well incorporated, about 1 minutes. Increase the speed to medium and beat until the frosting lightens and is fluffy, about 1 minute. Blend in the remaining milk and/or schnapps if the frosting seems too stiff.

KAHLUA GLAZE

2 Tablespoons butter, softened
3/4 cup confectioners' sugar, sifted
1 Tablespoon Kahlua

Beat together until smooth. If too dry, add a little more Kahlua.

PORTLY CRANBERRY SAUCE

1 (12 oz) package fresh cranberries
1 ½ cups sugar
3/4 cup orange juice
½ cup port wine
2 tsp grated orange peel

In small saucepan, combine all ingredients, except orange peel. Bring to a boil. Reduce heat and simmer for 30 minutes or until cranberries are popping and soft and mixture is slightly thickened. Remove from heat and stir in orange peel. Sauce will thicken more as it cools.

Makes 2 cups

PEACH JAM SAUCE

3 cups fresh peaches, peeled, chopped (divided)
1/4 cup white grape juice
2 Tablespoons brown sugar, packed
2 Tablespoons coffee liqueur
3 Tablespoons spiced rum
1 tsp lemon juice
pinch salt

In skillet, over medium heat, combine 2 cups of the peaches, the grape juice, brown sugar, coffee liqueur, spice rum, lemon jice, and salt. Mix well. Bring to a boil.

Boil for 3 minutes. Reduce the heat to low and simmer for 10 minutes, stirring frequently.

When the mixture thickens, remove from the heat. Pour it into a bowl. Add the remaining 1 cup of peaches and let cool slightly before serving.

Store extra sauce in an airtight container in the refrigerator.

PLUM JAM SAUCE

4 cups plums, peeled, pitted, and chopped (divided)
1/3 cup honey
½ cup white grape juice
1/3 cup spiced rum
2 Tablespoons red wine
1 Tablespoon fresh lemon juice
1 Tablespoon fresh lime juice
pinch salt

In skillet, over medium heat, combine 2 cups of the plums, the honey, grape juice, rum, wine, lemon and lime juices, and salt. Mix well. Bring to a boil.

Boil 3 minutes. Add another 1 cup of plums. Return to a boil. Reduce the heat to low and simmer to reduce the liquid, stirring frequently, about 10 minutes.

When thickened, remove from heat. Pour into bowl. Add remaining 1 cup of plums and let cool. Store an extra sauce in an airtight container in the refrigerator.

CHOCOLATE SAUCE FOR ICE CREAM

½ cup heavy cream
1/4 cup sugar
1 Lindt chocolate bar
2 Tablespoons unsalted butter
2 Tablespoons liqueur Irish cream or Kahlua

In microwave bowl, melt butter and chocolate bar. Stir. Add sugar and heavy cream and whisk until smooth. Add liqueur and stir. Serve warm over ice cream.

RASPBERRY JAM SAUCE

4 cups fresh raspberries (divided)
1/4 cup honey
2 Tablespoons white grape juice
3 Tablespoons spiced rum
1 tsp fresh lime juice
2 tsp vanilla
pinch salt

In skillet, over medium heat, combine 2 cups of the raspberries, the honey, grape juice, rum, lime juice, vanilla, and salt. Mix well. Bring to a boil.

Boil 3 minutes. Add 1 cup of raspberries. Reduce heat to medium low and simmer to reduce the liquid (about 10 minutes), stirring frequently. When the mixture thickens, remove from heat. Add the remaining 1 cup raspberries and let cool. Store any extra sauce in an airtight container in the refrigerator.

PECAN BOURBON CARAMEL SAUCE

1 cup sugar
3/4 cup heavy cream
3 Tablespoons bourbon
1 tsp fresh lemon juice
1 cup pecans, toasted, chopped

In a saucepan, cook sugar over moderately low heat, swirling pan occasionally, until melted and pale golden. Remove pan from heat and carefully add cream, bourbon, lemon juice, and pecans (caramel will steam and harden). Return pan to heat and simmer sauce, stirring, until caramel is dissolved, about 5 minutes. Pour sauce into bowl and cool. Sauce keeps, covered and chilled, 2 weeks.

Makes about 1 ½ cups.

STRAWBERRY JAM SAUCE

3 cups fresh strawberries, chopped
1/4 cup honey
1/4 cup white grape juice
1/3 cup spiced rum
2 Tablespoons red wine
1 tsp fresh lemon juice
pinch salt

In skillet, over medium heat, combine 2 cups of the strawberries, the honey, grape juice, rum, red wine, lemon juice, and salt. Mix well. Bring to a boil.

Boil for 3 minutes. Reduce the heat to low and simmer to reduce the liquids, stirring frequently (about 10 minutes). When the mixture thickens, remove from heat. Pour into a bowl. Add the remaining 1 cup of strawberries and let cool. Store any extra sauce in an airtight container in the refrigerator.

ORANGE BRANDY SAUCE

2 Tablespoons Brandy
1 Cup orange marmalade
1 cup orange juice
1/4 cup brown sugar
1 cup raisins
pinch of salt

In saucepan, combine all ingredients. Simmer 10 minutes.

Makes 3 cups

Refrigerate leftovers.

BOURBON STEAK MARINADE

3/4 cup brown sugar, packed
1 cup bourbon
1 cup pineapple juice
1/3 cup soy sauce
4 cups water

In large bowl, combine bourbon and brown sugar. Stir to dissolve sugar. Add pineapple juice, soy sauce, and water. Stir. Place steaks in 9 x 13 baking pan. Pour marinade over steaks and cover with plastic wrap. Let sit overnight in refrigerator. Over-marinating may cause the meat to dehydrate and toughen.

Cook over indirect heat, not directly over coals.

SOUR CHERRY SAUCE

1 onion, halved, then sliced
1 ½ Tablespoons oil
2 Tablespoons sugar
1/4 cup red-wine vinegar
8 oz pitted sour cherries, thawed (reserving any juice)
½ cup ruby Port

In heavy skillet over medium-low heat, cook onion in the oil, stirring occasionally, until golden brown, 15-20 minutes. Sprinkle sugar over onions and cook, stirring occasionally until sugar is caramelized and onion is deep golden, about 5 minutes. Add vinegar and oil, stirring, until reduced to a thick glaze, about 1 minute. Add cherries, with juice, and Port. Boil, stirring, until slightly syrupy, 6 - 8 minutes.

Serve with pork or chicken.

BOURBON BBQ SAUCE

1 small onion
4 garlic cloves, minced
3/4 cup bourbon
½ tsp pepper
2 tsp salt
6 oz can tomato paste
1/3 cup cider vinegar
1/4 cup Worcestershire sauce
½ cup brown sugar
2 cups ketchup

In large skillet over medium heat, combine onion garlic, and bourbon. Saute for 10 minutes, or until onion is translucent. Add remaining ingredients. Mix well and bring to boil. Reduce heat and simmer for 20 minutes. Puree in blender.

Makes 4 cups - best if made a day or two ahead of use

BURGUNDY MARINADE

(For 2 lbs. of Beef)

½ tsp salt
1/4 tsp pepper
1 garlic clove, minced
½ cup oil
½ cup burgundy
2 Tablespoons ketchup
2 Tablespoons molasses

In 12 x 8 inch baking dish or large plastic bag, combine all marinade ingredients. Mix well. Add steak; turn to coat. Cover dish or seal bag. Tender steaks should marinate *no more than* 2 hours. Less tender steaks, such as chuck and top round, *at least 3 hours* or overnight in refrigerator, turning occasionally. Discard remaining marinade.

RED WINE SWEET BARBECUE SAUCE

1 cup red wine
1 cup tomatoes, pureed
1 red onion, diced
2 Tablespoons tomato paste
1/4 cup molasses
3 Tablespoons brown sugar, packed
3 Tablespoons coffee liqueur
2 Tablespoons red wine vinegar
1 Tablespoon lemon pepper
1 ½ Tablespoon Worcestershire sauce
1/4 tsp cayenne pepper

In large saucepan, combine all ingredients. Bring to a boil over medium heat. Boil gently for about 5 minutes, stirring frequently. Reduce heat to low, cover, and simmer for 1 hour, stirring frequently. Store in airtight container in the refrigerator.
Makes about 2 ½ cups

ORANGE-PLUM BARBECUE SAUCE

2 (12 oz) cans frozen orange juice concentrate, thawed
2 (12 oz) jars plum preserves
½ cup honey
½ cup tomato paste
1/4 cup dry sherry
2 Tablespoons ginger, minced
2 Tablespoons soy sauce
2 garlic cloves, minced
½ tsp salt
½ tsp pepper

In large saucepan, combine all ingredients. Heat over medium-high heat until mixture begins to simmer, stirring occasionally. Reduce heat to medium-low and simmer 10 minutes. Cover and remove from heat. Cool 30 minutes. Spoon into 4 labeled 12 oz. containers. Store refrigerated up to 3 weeks or freeze.

CRANBERRY AND PORT SAUCE

1 (12 oz) package fresh cranberries
1 ½ cups sugar
3/4 cup orange juice
½ cup port wine
2 tsp grated orange peel

In small saucepan, stir together all ingredients except orange peel. Bring to a boil. Reduce heat and simmer, uncovered, for 30 minutes or until cranberries are popping and soft and mixture is slightly thickened (it will continue to thicken as it cools). Stir in orange peel. Makes 2 cups

Serving suggestions: with turkey, chicken, pork, vanilla ice cream, cheesecake

BALSAMIC POPPY SEED DRESSING

2 Tablespoons Balsamic vinegar
1 Tablespoon poppy seeds
½ tsp dry mustard
2 Tablespoons white wine
1 green onion - white part only - minced
2 Tablespoons orange juice
1 tsp sugar
1/4 tsp salt
2 Tablespoons olive oil

Combine, shake well and drizzle over green salad.

Vegetables

Be happy, young man, while you are young, and let your heart give you joy
in the days of your youth. Follow the ways of your heart and whatever
your eyes see, but know that for all these things
God will bring you to judgement.

Ecclesiastes 11: 9

ASPARAGUS WITH BEER AND HONEY SAUCE

1 lb fresh asparagus, washed and ends trimmed
½ tsp crushed thyme leaves
½ cup dark beer or larger beer, room temperature
1/3 cup Dijon mustard
1 garlic clove, minced
1/3 cup honey
1/4 tsp pepper
½ tsp salt

In saucepan large enough for asparagus to lay flat, boil about 1 inch of water, with a bit of salt. Add asparagus to boiling water, cover, cook about 2 - 3 minutes or until crisp-tender. Drain.

Meanwhile, in a small saucepan, combine thyme, beer, mustard, honey, garlic, thyme, pepper and salt. Heat over medium-high heat, stirring occasionally, just until boiling. Pour sauce over hot, cooked asparagus.

Serves 4

BOURBON CARROTS

1/4 cup butter
5 medium carrots, peeled and sliced into thin rounds
1 onion, thinly sliced
2 Tablespoons bourbon
1 tsp brown sugar

In heavy skillet, melt butter over medium-low heat. Add carrots and onion and cook 5 minutes, stirring often. Mix in bourbon and sugar. Cover and cook until carrots are tender, stirring occasionally, about 5 minutes.

DRUNKEN BEANS

8 bacon slices, cut into 1 inch pieces

1 lb dried pinto beans
5 ½ cups water
2 onions, chopped
8 large garlic cloves, minced
1 12-oz bottle dark beer, room temperature
4 tsp ground cumin
1 Tablespoon ground coriander
1 Tablespoon sugar
1 Tablespoon chili powder

3 plum tomatoes, chopped
salt and pepper to taste

Cook bacon in heavy large pot over medium-high heat until brown and almost crisp. Drain on paper towel. Discard bacon grease. Return bacon to pot. Place beans in same pot. Add water, onions and garlic; boil 15 minutes. Reduce heat to medium. Add beer, cumin, coriander, sugar, and chili powder. Cover partially and simmer 1 hour.

Add tomatoes to beans, cover partially and simmer 45 minutes. Uncover, simmer until beans are tender and mixture is thick, about 20 minutes. Season with salt and pepper.

6 servings

BOURBON YAMS WITH PECAN TOPPING

3 (1 lb. 13 oz) cans yams in light syrup, drained
3 eggs, beaten
1 stick butter, melted
½ cup whipping cream
2 Tablespoons bourbon
1 tsp vanilla

Pecan Topping:
1 stick butter, melted
1 cup pecans, chopped
1 cup brown sugar
1 cup flour

Preheat oven to 350 degrees. Butter casserole dish.

Mash yams. Add eggs, butter, cream, bourbon and vanilla. Stir well. Pour into buttered casserole. Topping: Combine all topping ingredients and sprinkle over yams. Bake uncovered 40 minutes, until heated through and top is lightly browned.

CROCKED CARROTS

1 lb baby carrots
1 Tablespoon butter
1 cup beer, room temperature
1/4 tsp salt
1 tsp brown sugar

Rinse and cut baby carrots into quarters. In skillet, melt butter. Add beer and carrots. Cook over low heat until tender, stirring frequently. Stir in salt and sugar. Cook for an additional 2 - 3 minutes. Serve.

Serves 4 - 6

CARROTS IN BEER

1 lb carrots, peeled and sliced
1 Tablespoon butter
1 cup dark lager beer, room temperature
1 tsp parsley flakes
1/4 tsp salt
1/4 tsp pepper
1 tsp sugar

In medium saucepan, bring beer to a soft boil. Add carrots. Reduce heat and cook until fork-tender. Drain.

In small saucepan, melt butter. Add parsley flakes, sugar, salt and pepper. Stir and cook for 1 minute. Pour over carrots and toss to coat.

Serves 4

BOURBON PECAN SMASHED SWEET POTATOES

3 medium sweet potatoes, peeled and cut into chunks
3 Tablespoons butter, softened, chopped
½ cup chopped pecans
3 Tablespoons brown sugar
1/4 cup bourbon
½ cup orange juice
1/4 tsp ground nutmeg
salt & pepper to taste

In medium saucepan, boil sweet potatoes in water until very tender, about 12-15 minutes. Drain. Cover and set aside. In small saucepan, over medium heat, melt butter. Add nuts and toast for 2 minutes, stirring occasionally. Stir in sugar. When it bubbles, add bourbon. Cook one minute. Stir in orange juice and nutmeg. Remove from heat. Mash potatoes. Stir in bourbon mixture. Salt and pepper to taste.

Serves 4

WINE BAKED POTATOES

4 large potatoes, peeled and sliced
4 slices bacon, fried and broken into bits
1 cup cheddar cheese, shredded
4 Tablespoons chopped chives
½ cup chicken broth
½ cup white wine
salt and pepper

Preheat oven to 375 degrees. Grease casserole dish.

Arrange 1/3 of the sliced potatoes in the bottom of baking dish. Sprinkle with salt and pepper and then 1/3 of the bacon bits and 1/3 of the cheese. Repeat layers twice. In measuring cup, combine broth and wine. Pour over potatoes. Bake, uncovered for 1 hour or until potato slices are tender. Garnish with chives before serving.

BEER BATTERED VEGETABLES

1 1/3 cups flour
2 Tablespoons Parmesan cheese
1 Tablespoon parsley
1 tsp salt
1/8 tsp garlic powder
1 (12 oz) can beer, room temperature, flat
2 eggs, separated
vegetables: green peppers, cauliflower, onion, artichoke hearts, zucchini, broccoli - cut into bite-size pieces
Oil for deep-frying

With electric mixer, beat egg whites until stiff. In large bowl, combine flour, cheese, parsley, salt and garlic. Stir in beer and egg yolks. Fold egg whites into mixture. Dip vegetable pieces into batter. Fry in 375 degree oil, a few pieces at a time, until golden. Drain on paper toweling. Serve immediately.

BLACK BEANS AND RICE WITH CORN SALSA

14 oz. package dried black beans
1 large yellow onion, chopped
1 small green bell pepper, seeded, de-ribbed, diced

12 oz frozen corn, thawed
2 jalapeno chili peppers, seeded, minced
2 Tablespoons lime juice
½ cup red onion, finely chopped
1/3 cup cilantro, chopped
salt and fresh ground pepper to taste

1/4 cup olive oil
3 garlic cloves, finely chopped
1/4 cup fresh parsley, chopped
3/4 cup cilantro, chopped
1 Tablespoon brown sugar
2 tsp ground cumin
1 ½ tsp salt
1 ½ tsp dried oregano
3/4 cup dry white wine

2 cups water
1 cup basmati rice, rinsed and drained.

Beans: Rinse black beans; discard any stones or mis-shapened beans. Drain. Place in large bowl. Add water to cover by 2 inches. Let soak for 1 hour; drain. Re-cover with fresh water and soak another 2 hours.

Drain beans and place in large saucepan with yellow onion, bell pepper and water to cover by 2 inches. Bring to a boil over high heat. Reduce heat to medium-low and simmer, uncovered, until the beans are tender, about 1 hour. Remove from heat. Do not drain.

Salsa: In medium bowl, combine corn, chili peppers, lime juice, red onion, 1/3 cup cilantro and salt and pepper to taste. Mix well and set aside.

Beans Part 2: In large frying pan over medium-low heat, warm the olive oil. Add the garlic, parsley, 3/4 cup cilantro, brown sugar, cumin, oregano, 1 tsp salt and pepper to taste. Saute, stirring occasionally, until the garlic is golden, about 10 minutes. Remove from heat.

Rice: In a heavy saucepan, bring the 2 cups water and ½ tsp salt to a boil. Add the rice, stir once, cover, reduce to low heat and cook for 20 minutes. Check to see if the rice is tender and the water is absorbed. In not, re-cover and cook for a few minutes longer.

Beans Part 3: Meanwhile, add the white wine to the garlic mixture in frying pan and simmer over high heat until the wine is reduced ay 1/4, about 5 minutes. Reduce to medium heat. Add the beans and their cooking liquid and simmer, uncovered, until the liquid has evaporated, about 15 minutes.

Spoon the rice into individual bowls. Top with beans and then salsa. Serve immediately.

MAPLE WHISKEY GLAZED CARROTS

2 lb carrots, peeled, cut into rounds or thin sticks
1 tsp Dijon mustard
½ tsp salt
1/8 tsp ground black pepper
½ cup maple syrup
1 clove garlic, minced
1 tsp fresh rosemary leaves
1/4 cup whiskey

In large saucepan, bring water to boil. Add the carrots and cook until just tender, about 5 minutes. Drain and return carrots to saucepan.

Meanwhile, in small saucepan, over medium heat, combine the mustard, salt pepper, maple syrup, garlic and rosemary. Bring to a simmer and cook for 5 minutes. Remove pan from heat and slowly stir in whiskey. Return pan to heat and simmer for another 10 minutes, or until thick and syrupy. Pour over carrots and gently toss to coat.

Serves 6 - 8

COWBOY BEANS

2 cans (15 oz) pinto beans, drained and rinsed
3/4 cup beer
½ cup finely chopped onion
½ cup coarsely chopped ham or 4-5 slices crisp-cooked bacon, crumbled
1 can (4oz) diced green chili peppers
1/3 cup molasses
1/4 cup catsup
1 Tablespoon chili powder

Preheat over to 350 degrees.

In a 1 ½-quart casserole, combine all ingredients. Stir to mix thoroughly. Bake, uncovered, for 1 - 1 ½ hrs. or until desired consistency. Stir occasionally.

WHITE WINE AND SHALLOT POTATO SALAD

½ cup finely chopped shallots
1/3 cup dry white wine
3 Tablespoons white wine vinegar
3 lb hot cooked small (2-inch) boiling potatoes, quartered
1/3 cup chopped flat-leaf parsley
1/4 cup olive oil
1 ½ tsp salt
½ tsp pepper

In large bowl, mix shallots, wine, vinegar, and salt. Add hot potatoes. Toss to coat. Let stand until cooled to warm, about 30 minutes. Stir in parsley, oil and pepper. Serve warm or at room temperature.

Serves 6

KENTUCKY SWEET POTATOES

3 lbs large sweet potatoes, peeled and quartered
1 cup light brown sugar, packed
1/4 tsp salt
½ stick unsalted butter
1/4 cup water
1/4 cup bourbon

Preheat oven to 375 degrees.

In steamer pan, with lid, steam potatoes over boiling water to fork tender. Transfer to buttered 3-quart casserole dish.
Meanwhile, in small saucepan, mix brown sugar, butter, water, and salt.
Bring to a simmer, stirring occasionally, until sugar is dissolved and syrup is thickened - about 5 minutes. Stir in bourbon. Drizzle syrup over potatoes and bake about 1 1/4 hours, until syrup is thickened, basting occasionally.

Serves 6

BROCCOLI IN WINE SAUCE

1 Tablespoon butter
2 tsp olive oil
2 cloves garlic, finely chopped
½ cup dry white wine
½ cup fresh orange juice
2 Tablespoons freshly grated orange peel

3 lbs broccoli, large stalks trimmed and split lengthwise

In small saucepan, melt the butter . Add the oil and garlic. Saute for 3 - 4 minutes, stirring frequently. Add the wine, orange juice and orange peel. Reduce the mixture over high heat until thick and syrupy (about 6 - 8 minutes), stirring frequently.

Meanwhile, steam the broccoli, covered, in steamer pan, until tender.

Put broccoli in serving dish and pour sauce over. Serve immediately.

Serves 4 - 6

ROASTED GARLIC WINE MASHED POTATOES

8 cloves garlic, peeled, quartered lengthwise
2 Tablespoons olive oil
2 Tablespoons white wine
8 large Russet potatoes, washed, peeled, cut into 1-inch cubes
5 Tablespoons butter
1 tsp salt
1/4 tsp white pepper
3/4 cup fat-free half-and-half

Preheat oven to 400 degrees.

In small baking dish, combine oil, wine, and garlic. Bake until garlic is deep golden brown, about 15 minutes.

In large saucepan, put potatoes and enough water to cover potatoes plus one inch. Add 1 teaspoon salt. Bring water to a boil over medium-high heat. Reduce heat to a soft boil, partially cover pot with lid, and cook until potatoes are tender, about 20 minutes. Drain potatoes and return to pot.

Mash potatoes. Add the cream, butter, salt and pepper. Mash in. Mash the garlic with any remaining liquid from baking. Mash into the potato mixture until incorporated. Stir to smooth.

KAHLUA GLAZED CARROTS

3 cups carrots, sliced
1 Tablespoon butter
1 Tablespoon brown sugar
1 Tablespoon honey
3 Tablespoons Kahlua
1 tsp corn starch
1/4 tsp salt
3 slices bacon, cooked and crumbles
1 Tablespoon fresh parsley, chopped

Steam carrots over a small amount of boiling water. Cover and steam 4 - 5 minutes or just until tender. Remove from heat.

In large skillet, melt butter, over medium heat. Stir in bown sugar, honey, and 2 Tablespoons Kahlua. Cook over medium heat until bubbly. In small bowl, combine the cornstarch and remaining 1 Tablespoon of Kahlua. Stir well and add to brown sugar mixture, stirring as it is poured together. Stir in salt. Continue cooking until thickened and bubbly, stirring constantly. Add carrots, tossing to coat. Cook just until the carrots are thoroughly heated. Spoon into serving dish and sprinkle with crumbled bacon and chopped parsley.

Serves 6

GRAND MARNIER SWEET POTATOES

3 - 4 sweet potatoes, peeled, cubed
½ cup brown sugar
1/4 cup butter
1/4 cup raisins
1/4 cup water
3 Tablespoons Grand Marnier

Boil potatoes to fork tender. Drain. Slice.

Preheat oven to 350 degrees. Grease 9 x 13 baking dish.

In small saucepan, combine sugar, butter, raisins and water. Bring to a boil. Add Grand Marnier.

Fan potatoes in baking dish. Pour sauce over potatoes. Bake uncovered 30 minutes, basting occasionally.

Serves 6

THREE BEAN BOURBON BAKE

2 strips bacon

2 Tablespoons olive oil

1 large onion, chopped

1 small sweet green pepper, chopped

1 can (16 oz) petite diced tomatoes

½ cup molasses

6 Tablespoons tomato paste

1/3 cup bourbon

1/4 cup firmly packed light brown sugar

2 Tablespoons Dijon mustard

½ tsp salt

1/4 tsp black pepper

1 can(19 oz) black beans, drained, rinsed

1 can (19 oz) light red kidney beans, drained and rinsed

1 can (19 oz) dark kidney beans, drained and rinsed

Heat oven to 350 degrees.

In large skillet, cook bacon until crisp. Remove to paper towel to drain. Discard bacon fat. In same pan, add the olive oil. Heat. Add the onion and green pepper to skillet and saute 8 - 10 minutes or until tender. Stir in tomatoes, molasses, tomato paste, bourbon, brown sugar, mustard, salt and black pepper. Bring to boil, stirring occasionally, reduce heat and simmer 3-5 minutes.

Grease a large casserole dish. Pour in beans. Crumble in bacon. Pour sauce over, and stir to mix. Bake 45 minutes or until hot and bubbly.

BRANDIED ACORN SQUASH

1 acorn squash
1 Granny Smith Apple, chopped
1/4 cup chopped pecans
1 Tablespoon brown sugar
½ cup brandy

Cut acorn squash in half, lengthwise. Remove seed and membranes. Poke several holes in squash interior with fork. Place cut side up, in microwave dish with 1/4 cup water.

In bowl, mix remaining ingredients and place ½ in each cavity of squash. Lightly cover with waxed paper.

Microwave on high for 8-10 minutes or until tender.

Serves 2

TIPSY SWEET POTATOES

2 ½ cups cooked, mashed sweet potatoes
4 Tablespoons butter, softened
½ cup firmly packed light brown sugar
1/3 cup whiskey
½ cup pecan pieces
½ bag miniature marshmallows

Preheat oven to 325 degrees. Grease 1-qt casserole.

While potatoes are still hot and newly mashed, add butter, brown sugar, pecans, and whiskey. Stir well. Spoon into casserole dish. Top with marshmallows. Bake for 20-25 minutes until bubbly.

Serves 6 - 8

AMARETTO ALMOND CARROTS

1/4 cup slivered almonds
1 lb carrots, peeled, sliced 1/8-inch thick
2 Tablespoons butter
1/4 cup amaretto liqueur
1/4 cup water
1/8 tsp ground cinnamon
salt and white pepper to taste

Lightly toast slivered almonds in a dry skillet until fragrant. Set aside.

In heavy sauce pan, melt butter. Add amaretto, water, cinnamon, and carrots. Cover and simmer until carrots are just tender, but not overcooked. Salt and pepper to taste. Stir in toasted almonds.

Serves 6

POTATO SALAD

6 medium potatoes, peeled, quartered
1 medium sweet onion, chopped
2 celery stocks, chopped
3 hard boiled eggs, chopped
1 cup mayonnaise
½ cup sour cream
3 Tablespoons red wine
3 Tablespoons sugar
2 Tablespoons prepared mustard
salt and pepper to taste

Boil the potatoes about 20 minutes or until fork tender. Drain. Rinse in cold water. Cool to room temperature. Cut to desired size. In large bowl, combine mayonnaise, sour cream, wine, sugar, mustard, salt and pepper. Add onions and celery. Stir well. Add potatoes and stir. Fold in eggs. Taste. Add additional salt or pepper, if needed. Refrigerate several hours before serving.

SCOTCH ALE POTATOES

1 cup Scotch ale

1/4 cup olive oil

2 Tablespoons chopped fresh rosemary

2 Tablespoons chopped shallots

2 cloves garlic, chopped

4 large red potatoes, washed and cut into about 1 x 2 inch pieces

1 onion, peeled and cut into wedges

salt and pepper to taste

1/4 cup grated Parmesan cheese

In large freezer bag, combine Scotch ale, olive oil, rosemary, shallots, and garlic. Seal and squish to mix. Add potatoes and onions to the bag. Squeeze out the air and seal. Let marinate at room temperature for 1 hour, turning bag once or twice.

Preheat oven to 425 degrees. Line a roasting pan with aluminum foil.

Scoop out potatoes and onions from the freezer bag, reserving marinade. Place in a single layer in roasting pan. Spoon about 1/4 cup of marinade over the potatoes. Strain remaining marinade and top potatoes with solids. Cover pan. Bake for 30 minutes. Uncover potatoes. Stir. Sprinkle with cheese. Return to the oven, uncovered, for 15 minutes, or until browned and tender. Let potatoes rest 5 minutes before serving.

GREEN BEANS WITH GARLIC AND VODKA

1 Tablespoon soy sauce
1 Tablespoon vodka
1 tsp sugar
oil, for frying
1 ½ lb green beans, washed and trimmed
1 Tablespoon garlic, minced
1 tsp dried red chili pepper flakes

In small mixing bowl, combine soy sauce, vodka and sugar. Stir. Set aside.

In wok, heat the oil. Fry the green beans in several batches, for about 20 seconds each batch. Drain on paper towel. Discard all, but about 2 Tablespoons of oil.

Turn the heat to high and stir-fry the garlic and red pepper for 10-15 seconds. Return the beans to the wok and stir-fry to coat with the garlic.

Add the vodka mixture and stir-fry for a few seconds until the beans are well coated. Transfer the beans to a serving dish. Pour any remaining sauce over the beans. Serve immediately.

Serves 6

PECAN BRANDIED CARROTS

½ cup pecan pieces
2 Tablespoons butter
1 (16 oz) frozen baby carrots
1/4 cup honey
3 Tablespoons orange juice
3 Tablespoons brandy
1 tsp cornstarch

In large dry skillet over medium high heat, toast pecans for 5-6 minutes, stirring frequently; Set nuts aside.

In same skillet over medium heat, melt butter. Add carrots and cook for 4-5 minutes, stirring occasionally. Add honey, orange juice, and brandy. Cook covered, stirring occasionally for 10-12 minutes or until carrots are tender. Transfer 2 Tablespoons liquid from skillet to small dish. Stir in cornstarch until dissolved. Stir cornstarch mixture into carrots. Cook an additional 2 minutes or until sauce is thickened and carrots are glazed. Stir in pecans. Makes 6 - 8 servings.

SNOW PEAS WITH GRAND MARNIER

1 cup water
1 tsp sugar
3 (10oz) packages frozen snow peas
1 (8oz) can sliced water chestnuts, drained
1/4 cup Grand Marnier
5 Tablespoons butter
dash of salt

2 Tablespoons chopped fresh mint leaves,
OR 1 ½ Tablespoon dried mint

In large saucepan, bring 1 cup water to boil and add the sugar. Add the snow peas and cook until barely tender. Drain. Return to pan. Add the water chestnuts, Grand Marnier, butter, mint and dash of salt. Cook over medium-low heat until heated through. Serves 8

Entrees

He makes grass grow for the cattle, and plants for man to cultivate - bringing forth food from the earth: wine that gladdens the heart of man, oil to make his face shine, and bread that sustains his heart.

Psalm 104:14-15

TEQUILA PORK TENDERLOIN

oil for browning
3 garlic cloves, chopped
2 lbs pork tenderloin, fat removed
1/4 cup Dijon mustard
1 small onion, chopped
1 small carrot, diced
½ celery stock, diced
1 can (14.5 oz) petite diced tomatoes, not drained
juice of 1 lime
1 tsp thyme
½ tsp pepper
1 bay leaf
1 tsp chili powder
1/4 to ½ cup tequila
salt and pepper to taste

With hands, coat pork with mustard. In large skillet, heat oil and garlic. Over medium heat, brown mustard-coated pork. Add remaining ingredients. Stir to combine. Heat to boiling; reduce heat. Cover and simmer until pork in done, about 30 minutes. Remove bay leaf. Let pork rest for about 15 minutes, then slice.

Serves 4-6

SLOW COOKER BEEF BOURGUIGNONNE

1 lb boneless beef chuck roast, cut into 3/4 inch cubes
2 Tablespoons flour
2 Tablespoons olive oil
1 onion, chopped
1 garlic clove, minced
3 cups whole fresh mushrooms
4 medium carrots, cut into 3/4 inch pieces
2 cups frozen small whole pearl onions
3 Tablespoons quick-cooking tapioca
1 tsp dried thyme, crushed
3/4 tsp dried marjoram, crushed
½ tsp salt
1/4 tsp pepper
2 bay leaves
1 1/4 cup Burgundy
½ cup beef broth
1/4 cup cold water

2 slices bacon, crisp-cooked, crumbled
3 cups hot cooked noodles

In large skillet, heat 1 Tablespoon oil. Dredge meat in flour. Brown ½ of the meat, chopped onion and garlic. Cook until meat is browned and onion is tender. Remove meat from pan. Add remaining 1 Tablespoon oil; brown remaining ½ of meat, onion and garlic. Brown as before. Drain off fat.

In large slow cooker, layer mushrooms, carrots, and pearl onions. Sprinkle with tapioca. Place meat mixture on top of vegetables. Add thyme, marjoram, salt, and pepper, and bay leaves. Pour in Burgundy and beef broth and water. Cover and cook on low heat for 10 - 12 hours or until vegetables are tender. Discard bay leaves. Stir in bacon. Serve with noodles.

VIRGINIA BAY SCALLOPS IN WINE SAUCE

3/4 cup bread crumbs

1/4 cup Parmesan cheese

6 Tablespoons butter

2 celery stalks, slices

1 onion, thinly sliced

6 Tablespoons flour

1 cup milk

½ cup white wine

4 oz medium-sharp Cheddar cheese, shredded

1 lb Virginia Bay scallops

Preheat oven to 350 degrees. Grease 2qt. casserole dish.

In medium saucepan, melt butter. Saute celery and onion. Blend in flour to make a paste; cook 1 full minute over medium heat. Gradually stir in milk. Stir in wine. Add Cheddar cheese and let melt into sauce, stirring frequently. Fold in scallops. Pour into casserole dish. In small bowl, combine bread crumbs and Parmesan cheese. Sprinkle over casserole. Bake for 20-30 minutes, until bubbly. Serve over noodle or rice.

ORANGE-CHILE CHICKEN WITH BLACK BEANS

4 Tablespoons olive oil, divided
3 - 4 lbs chicken pieces
1 large purple onion, halved, sliced thinly
4 garlic cloves, minced
1 ½ cup orange juice
3/4 cup low-sodium chicken stock
3 Tablespoons hot chile sauce
1 3/4 cups cooked black beans with 3 Tablespoons liquid
1 red bell pepper, but into strips
1 Tablespoon dark rum
salt and pepper to taste

In large skillet, heat 2 Tablespoons oil over medium heat. Saute onions until slightly browned. Add garlic and saute one minute. Remove from pan. Heat other 2 Tablespoons oil in same skillet. Brown chicken on all sides. Add onions and garlic. In bowl, combine orange juice, chicken stock, and chile sauce. Pour over chicken. Cover and simmer over low heat 30 minutes. Add black beans with liquid and bell pepper strips. Simmer, uncovered, 30 minutes. Add rum, salt and pepper; simmer 15 minutes.

SHREDDED BEEF BRISKET IN WINE

1 beef brisket (4 -5 lbs) cut into ½ inch cubes
½ cup olive oil, divided
2 carrot, peeled and chopped
1 celery stalk, diced
2 Tablespoons garlic, minced
1 onion, chopped
2 cups cabernet sauvignon wine
1 - 2 cups beef stock
1 bay leaf
2 Tablespoons dried thyme
½ cup cognac

In skillet, heat half the oil. Brown meat, lightly salting and peppering as it browns. Remove and set aside.

In same pan, add remaining oil. Brown carrots, celery, garlic and onion. Remove from heat and add 1/3 cup wine. Stir.

In stock pot, combine brisket, vegetables and juices. Add remaining wine, beef stock, bay leaf, thyme, and all except 2 Tablespoons of the cognac. Add salt and pepper to taste. Cover and cook until meat is tender (about 2 hours). Remove the meat and using 2 forks, shred the beef.

Meanwhile, reduce sauce, over low heat, uncovered, until thick enough to coat a spoon. Remove bay leaf. Return shredded brisket to the sauce. Add remaining cognac and serve the meat mounded up on a platter.

Serves 6 - 8

CHICKEN CREPES

2 ½ Tablespoons butter
1 ½ Tablespoons minced onions
2 ½ Tablespoons flour
1 ½ cups half and half
1 cup diced cooked chicken
1/4 cup sherry
1/4 cup grated parmesan
1/4 cup swiss gruyere
1/4 cup sliced almonds

In skillet, melt butter, add onions and saute until soft. Add flour; cook until bubbly, and add half and half. Cook until thick and creamy. Add chicken and sherry. Place 2 Tablespoons in each crepe and roll. Place in buttered shallow casserole. Cover with remaining sauce. Sprinkle with cheese and almonds. Bake at 425 degrees until brown.

Basic Crepe Recipe

1 cup flour
2 eggs
1 Tablespoon melted butter
1 3/4 cups milk
½ tsp salt

Mix flour and eggs well. Add remaining ingredients. Brush a 4 or 6 inch skillet with butter. Pour on 1 Tablespoon batter. Tilt pan to cover bottom. Cook quickly on both sides. Add more milk for thinner batter.
Serves 4

DRUNKEN SPARERIBS

1/4 cup bourbon
1/4 cup soy sauce
1/4 cup brown sugar
1 Tablespoon Dijon mustard
1 Tablespoon ketchup
4 lbs spareribs

Preheat oven to 350 degrees

In medium bowl, whisk together bourbon, soy sauce, brown sugar, mustard, and ketchup. Spread evenly on both sides of spareribs, reserving some sauce for basting during cooking. Place ribs on a rack in a deep roasting pan. Cover. Baste occasionally, with remaining sauce. Roast about 1 ½ hours, turning once, or until tender.

Serves 4

LEMONY CHICKEN

6 small boneless, skinless chicken breast halves
1/4 cup butter
½ cup Gerwurztraminer wine
1 Tablespoon lemon juice
1/4 tsp salt
2 Tablespoons sliced green onions, with tops
½ lemon, thinly slices
1/8 tsp dried dill weed

In large skillet, heat butter; cook chicken, turning once, until chicken is light brown; about 5 minutes on each side.

Mix wine, lemon juice, salt and dill weed; pour over chicken. Place lemon slices on chicken. Heat to boiling; reduce heat. Cover and simmer until chicken is done, 10 - 15 minutes. Remove chicken to warm platter; keep warm.

Heat wine mixture to boiling; cook until reduced by half, about 3 minutes. Pour over chicken; sprinkle with green onions.

BEER BATTER FISH

1 lb fish fillets
1/3 cup lemon juice
2/3 cup beer, room temperature
1 cup vegetable oil
1 ½ cups flour
2 1/4 tsp baking powder
3/4 tsp baking soda
1 ½ tsp salt

In large bowl, mix flour, baking powder, soda, and salt. Combine well. Divide in half, leaving half in the large bowl. Set second half aside. To the large bowl, add lemon juice and beer. Stir. Heat oil in large skillet over medium heat. Place fish on paper towels; pat dry. Coat fish in dry mix and then dip in beer batter. Fry until golden brown on both sides. Drain on paper towels.

BEER BRISKET

1 (4lb) beef brisket
1 large onion, slices
1 (12oz) beer
1 Tablespoon brown sugar
1 cube beef bouillon
2 Tablespoons coarsely ground black pepper
2 cloves garlic, minced
1 bay leaf
1/4 tsp dried thyme
2 Tablespoons cornstarch
2 Tablespoons water

Preheat oven to 350 degrees.

Line baking dish with aluminum foil. Place brisket in pan and cover with sliced onion. In medium bowl, mix together beer, brown sugar, bouillon, pepper, garlic, bay leaf, and thyme. Pour over roast. Cover with aluminum foil.

Bake for 4 hours, to fork-tender. Remove brisket from pan. Remove bay leaf. In small saucepan. Mix together the cornstarch and water. Stir in the meat juices. Stir and heat to make gravy.

SPAGHETTI WITH MEAT SAUCE

1 ½ lbs ground beef
1 onion, finely chopped
2 garlic cloves, finely chopped
3/4 tsp dried basil
½ tsp dried oregano
1 ½ tsp salt
½ tsp pepper
1/4 tsp sugar
3 (8oz) cans tomato sauce
1 (4 oz) mushroom stems and pieces, undrained
1 cup Zinfandel

1 (16 oz)package spaghetti
Grated Parmesan cheese

In large skillet, cook and stir ground beef, onion, and garlic until brown; drain. Stir in basil, oregano, salt, pepper, sugar, tomato sauce, and mushrooms. Heat to boiling; reduce heat. Cover and simmer 1 hour, stirring occasionally.

Stir in wine. Cover and simmer 30 minutes, stirring occasionally. Uncover and simmer 30 minutes longer, stirring occasionally. Prepare spaghetti as directed on package; drain, but do not rinse. Pour sauce over hot spaghetti. Serve with cheese.

CHICKEN L'ORANGE

2 - 2 ½ lbs chicken pieces, cleaned, skinned
1/4 cup flour
1 tsp salt
1/4 tsp pepper
4 Tablespoons butter
1 can (6 oz) frozen orange juice concentrate
1 cup white wine
1 can (8 oz) crushed pineapple, with juice
½ cup raisins
2 Tablespoons sugar
½ tsp cinnamon
½ tsp ground cloves
½ cup slivered almonds

Preheat over to 325 degrees

In shallow dish, mix together flour, salt and pepper. Dredge chicken to coat. In large skillet, melt butter over medium heat. Add chicken and cook, turning, about 10 minutes or until brown on all sides. Remove to shallow baking dish.

In large bowl, mix orange juice concentrate, wine, pineapple, raisins, sugar, cinnamon, and cloves. Pour over chicken. Sprinkle with almonds. Cover with aluminum foil. Bake, basting occasionally with pan liquid, for 30 minutes. Remove foil. Increase oven temperature to 350 degrees and bake about 15 minutes more, or until fork can be inserted in chicken with ease. Remove chicken to serving dish and pour sauce on top.

Serves 4

BEER BAKED BEANS & FRANKS

1 32-oz can baked beans
1 cup beer, room temperature
½ cup brewed coffee
½ cup chopped tomato
3/4 cup chopped onion
4 - 5 frankfurters, cut in 1-inch pieces
1 Tablespoon horseradish
½ cup catsup
½ cup molasses

Preheat oven to 325 degrees. In greased casserole dish, mix all ingredients, well. Bake for 1 hour, stirring occasionally. If beans appear to be frying out, add a small amount of additional beer.

Serves 6-8

SAVORY BEEF BRISKET

4 - 5 lbs beef brisket
1 packet dry onion soup mix
1/3 cup dry red wine

Preheat over to 325 degrees. Line 9 x 13 inch roasting pan with 3 layers of aluminum foil - cut large enough to mold and completely seal around the brisket like an envelope.
Blend soup mix with wine. Spoon ½ of soup mixture on foil; place brisket on top. Top with remaining soup mixture. Seal the foil over brisket.
Bake for 4 hours or until fork tender. Allow brisket to remain in unopened envelope for 15-20 minutes before removing to slice. Juices may be used au jus or thickened for gravy.

HAM - BEER - GRRR...

4 - 5 lbs ham (boneless)
1 Tablespoon whole cloves
½ cup maple syrup
2 tsp dry mustard
1 tsp black pepper
1 cup beer, room temperature
1 large onion, diced

Preheat oven to 325 degrees.

Score ham fat with knife by making cuts about 1 inch apart across diagonally and then cut across lines to form diamonds. This allows fat to render from the ham and provides greater surface area for the glaze to stick to. You may not be able to score a ham that has been "super trimmed" and has little fat left. Poke whole cloves into each diamond.

In bowl, mix remaining ingredients.

Line a roasting pan with aluminum foil and put in ham. Pour mixture over ham. Cover with foil and seal around edge of pan. Bake for approximately 1 hour per pound. Do not baste during cooking, as they tend to be too salty.

If you purchased a **fully cooked ham**, cook to 140 degrees internal temperature, about 15-20 minutes per pound.
If you purchased a **cook-before-eating ham**, cook to 160 degrees internal temperature, about 20-40 minutes per pound.

BEEF AND ONIONS IN BEER

2 lbs chuck or round roast, cut into 6 - 8 slices
2 Tablespoons butter
2 Tablespoons oil
1 large onion, peeled and thinly sliced
1 ½ tablespoons flour
2 cups dark beer, room temperature
1 tsp dried thyme
1 bay leaf

In large heavy Dutch oven, heat butter and olive oil. When hot, brown meat quickly on both sides. Remove beef and set aside.

Add sliced onions to the drippings. Lower heat and cook onions until lightly browned, stirring often. Add flour. Cook, stirring constantly, until the flour is lightly browned.

Add beer to pan, stirring until thickened. Add thyme and bay leaf. Return beef to the pot and cover. Cook over low heat about 2 ½ hours, until beef is tender. Check often to be sure the beef is covered in liquid, adding more beer or water if necessary. Remove bay leaf before serving.
Serve with butter noodles or rice

Serves 6 - 8

CHICKEN TARRAGON

2 - 2 ½ lbs chicken pieces, cleaned, skinned
½ cup flour
1 tsp salt
½ tsp pepper
1/4 cup butter
1/4 cup olive oil
1 onion, finely chopped
3 cloves garlic, chopped
1 tsp crushed tarragon leaves
1 cup white wine

Preheat oven to 350 degrees.

Combine flour, salt and pepper. Dredge chicken with flour mixture. In skillet, melt butter with olive oil. Add onion and garlic and saute until tender, but not brown. Remove onions and garlic from pan and set aside.

Brown chicken in skillet and place in a baking dish. Mix tarragon with the onions and garlic. Spread mixture over chicken. Pour wine over chicken. Cover with aluminum foil. Bake for 45 minutes, or until chicken is tender.

Serves 5-6

SLOW-COOKER POT ROAST

2 ½ - 3 lbs boneless beef chuck pot roast
2 Tablespoons cooking oil
3/4 cup dry red wine
1 Tablespoon Worcestershire sauce
1 tsp instant beef bouillon granules
1 tsp dried basil, crushed
2 medium potatoes, quartered
8 small carrots, sliced 1/4 inch
1 onion, cut into wedges
2 stalks celery, cut into 1 inch slices

½ cup cold water
1/4 cup flour

Trim fat from roast. Brown roast in 4 -6 qt pot on all sides in hot oil. Drain off fat. Place vegetables in large slow-cooker pot. Place roast on top of vegetables (cut to fit, if needed). Combine the 3/4 cup water, Worcestershire sauce, bouillon, and basil. Add to cooker. Cover and cook on low for 10 - 12 hours.

Gravy: Measure juices; skim off fat. If necessary, add enough water to juices to make 1 ½ cups liquid. In sauce pan, stir together the ½ cup cold water and flour. Stir in juices. Cook and stir over medium heat until thickened and bubbly. Cook and stir for 1 minute more. Season with salt and pepper.

CHIPOTLE ORANGE GLAZED PORK CHOPS

2 Tablespoons pure maple syrup
2 Tablespoons frozen orange juice concentrate, thawed
1 tsp chipotle chili sauce
2 Tablespoons tequila
4 center cut, pork chops
½ tsp salt
2 Tablespoons olive oil

In small bowl, mix maple syrup, orange juice concentrate and chipotle to create glaze.

In large skillet, heat oil, over medium high heat.

Sprinkle both sides of chops with salt. Brush one side generously with glaze. Carefully, to prevent oil from splattering, place chops in skillet, glazed side down. Brush other side with glaze. Cook, turning and glazing, until cooked through, about 5 minutes per side.

SLOW COOKER BEEF TIPS IN WINE

4 lbs sirloin tips, or eye of round, cubed
1 tsp salt
1 tsp pepper
½ cup flour

1 cup celery, chopped
1 tsp Worcestershire sauce
2 Tablespoons ketchup
10 oz. beef broth
1 garlic clove
1 onion, sliced thinly
8 oz can sliced mushrooms, drained
3 Tablespoons olive oil

3 Tablespoons flour
1/4 cup dry red wine

buttered noodles

Heat olive oil in skillet over medium-low heat. Combine salt, pepper and ½ cup flour. Toss beef cubes in mixture until coated. Brown meat on all sides. Do not drain. Place in bottom of large slow cooker. Add garlic, onion, mushrooms, and celery. Combine beef broth with Worcestershire sauce and ketchup. Pour over meat and vegetables; mix together well. Cover and cook on low for 5-6 hours.

One hour before serving, turn cooker to high. Make smooth paste of 3 Tablespoons flour and the wine. Stir into meat and vegetables; cook only until thickened. Serve over hot buttered noodles.
Serves 8 - 10

BEEF BRISKET WITH LEMON ONION

1 beef brisket (5 - 6 lbs)
2 medium onions, slices
2 lemons, thinly sliced
1 cup port wine
½ cup brown sugar, packed
1 Tablespoon dry marjoram leaves
1 tsp pepper

Preheat oven to 300 degrees

In large roasting pan, place onion slices and most of the lemon slices (reserving some for garnish). Lay brisket on top of onions and lemon. In bowl, mix together port, brown sugar, and marjoram. Stir until sugar dissolves. Pour evenly over brisket. Sprinkle with pepper and cover roasting pan tightly with aluminum foil. Bake until brisket is very tender when pierced, about 4 hours.

When brisket is tender, uncover pan and return it to the oven to brown the meat slightly, about 15 minutes.

Remove brisket to platter and keep warm. Let meat rest about 5 minutes before slicing across grain.

CHICKEN GRAND MARNIER

3/4 cup Grand Marnier
1 1/4 cup apricot jam
3/4 cup distilled white vinegar
4 ½ Tablespoons Worcestershire sauce
3 Tablespoons Dijon mustard
3 Tablespoons honey
1 Tablespoon dried red pepper flakes
6 boneless chicken breasts, skinned
olive oil

In microwave-safe bowl, combine Grand Marnier, jam, vinegar, Worcestershire sauce, mustard, honey, and red pepper flakes. Microwave for 1 minute or until the honey and jam are melted. Stir. Let cool to room temperature.

Place chicken breasts in a single layer in a shallow glass baking dish. Cover with plastic wrap and refrigerate at least 4 hours. Remove from refrigerator while preheating the oven.

Preheat oven to 350 degrees

Pour off all but about 3/4 cup marinade. Cover loosely with foil. Bake for 45 minutes to 1 hour, basting with marinade every 15 minutes.

Serves 6

BRISKET IN SWEET AND SOUR SAUCE

(For best flavor, cook brisket the day before serving)

1 medium onion, quartered
1 two-inch piece fresh ginger, peeled
6 garlic cloves
1/4 cup Dijon mustard
½ cup dry red wine
1 ½ cups cola or ginger ale
1 cup ketchup
1/4 cup honey
1/4 cup cider vinegar
1/4 cup soy sauce
½ cup olive oil
1/4 tsp groud cloves
1 Tablespoon pepper
1 6 to 7 lb brisket

Preheat oven to 350 degrees

In food processor, place onion, ginger, garlic, mustard, red wine, cola, ketchup, honey, vinegar, soy sauce, oil, cloves, and pepper. Process until smooth.

Place brisket, fat side up, into a heavy baking pan, just large enough to hold it, and pour sauce over it. Cover tightly and bake for 2 hours. Turn brisket over and bake uncovered for one more hour or until fork-tender. **Cool.** Cover brisket and refrigerate overnight in cooking pan.

The next day, preheat oven to 350 degrees. Transfer brisket to a cutting board, cut off fat and slice against grain, to desired thickness. Remove any congealed fat from sauce and bring to a boil in saucepan on stovetop. Put meat and sauce in clean baking pan and warm in oven for 20 minutes. Serve warm. Serves 12

GRILLED WHISKEY SALMON

4 8-oz salmon fillets, skinned, boned
½ cup whiskey
1/4 cup light soy sauce
1/4 cup orange juice
2 Tablespoons vegetable oil
2 garlic cloves, minced

In mixing bowl, combine whiskey, soy sauce, orange juice, oil and garlic.

Place fish in a shallow dish and pour mixture over. Cover with plastic wrap and refrigerate for 1 hour or more. Spray broiler pan with non-stick cooking spray. Remove salmon from marinade and discard marinade. Broil 5 minutes on each side. Salmon is done when it flakes easily and has faded in color.

Can be grilled, instead of broiling.

Serves 4 -6

APPLE-WINE CHICKEN

2 lbs chicken pieces
1/4 cup butter
2 Tablespoons apple jelly
6 Tablespoons dry white wine
1 tsp salt

Preheat oven to 350 degrees. In small saucepan, melt butter with apple jelly and wine. Place chicken in 13x9x2 baking dish. Pour the sauce over the chicken. Cover with aluminum foil and bake for 50 minutes.

Remove foil. Baste chicken with sauce. Return to oven to brown, about 10 minutes. Check chicken for doneness

BEEF BURGUNDY

2 ½ lbs beef boneless chuck, tip or round (about 1 inch thick)

1/4 cup vegetable oil

3 Tablespoons flour

2 tsp salt

2 tsp instant beef bouillon

1/4 tsp dried marjoram leaves

1/4 tsp dried thyme leaves

1/8 tsp pepper

1 1/4 cups Burgundy or other dry red wine

3/4 cup water

1 large onion, slices

8 oz mushrooms, cut into halves

Cut beef into large-bite-size pieces. (For easier cutting, partially freeze beef.) Heat oil in 4-qt Dutch oven. Cook and stir beef until brown; drain. In small bowl, mix dry ingredients together. Sprinkle dry mixture over beef. Stir in wine, water and onions. Heat to boiling; reduce heat. Cover and simmer until beef is tender, about 1 hour. Stir in mushrooms. Cover and simmer until mushrooms are done, 10-15 minutes.

HONEY PECAN CHICKEN

2 Tablespoons butter
1 Tablespoon minced shallots
1 cup orange juice
1/4 cup bourbon
1 cup whipping cream
1 Tablespoons honey
1 Tablespoon cider vinegar
salt and pepper to taste

Sauce: In medium saucepan, heat butter; add shallots and cook over low heat 3 - 4 minutes or until tender, but not brown. Add orange juice and bourbon, increase heat, and contine cooking until liquid is reduced to ½ cup. Add cream and reduce until slightly thickened. Add honey and vinegar and season with salt and pepper.

6 boneless, skinless chicken breast halves
1/4 cup flour
1 tsp thyme
1/4 cup finely chopped pecans
salt and pepper
Olive oil for sauteing

Chicken: Mix flour, thyme, pecans, salt, and pepper. Dredge chicken breasts in flour mixture. Heat small amount of oil in large skillet. Add chicken and saute until golden brown. If breasts are thick and large, cover pan after sauteing for 10 minutes, then remove lid and saute another 5 minutes or so. Pour sauce onto each plate and place chicken breast in center. Serve additional sauce separately. Serves 6

AMARETTO SALMON ORIENTAL

1/4 cup amaretto
2 Tablespoons light soy sauce
2 Tablespoons lime juice
2 Tablespoons sesame oil
1/4 tsp pepper
1/4 tsp ground ginger
salt to taste
2 (1 ½ lb each) salmon fillets, skinned, boned

In mixing bowl, combine amaretto, soy sauce, lime juice, sesame oil, pepper, ginger, and salt. In glass baking dish, marinade salmon in mixture for at least 1 hour.

Preheat over to 350 degrees.

Lightly spray a broiling pan with non-stick cooking spray. Remove salmon from marinade and discard marinade. Broil for about 5 minutes per side. Salmon should be flaky and faded in color.

Serves 4

BREWED BEEF ON NOODLES

4 Tablespoons oil
1 large onion, sliced
4 lbs boneless beef chuck, cut into 2-in cubes
3 Tablespoons flour
1 (12 oz) can of beer, room temperature
3/4 cup water
2 cubes beef bouillon
1 bay leaf
1 tsp sugar
1/4 tsp basil
½ tsp pepper

Hot cooked noodles

Preheat oven to 350 degrees. Line baking pan with aluminum foil.

In skillet, heat 2 Tablespoons oil, over medium heat. Add onions. Cook and stir until golden and tender. Remove onions, with slotted spoon, to baking pan. In skillet, brown meat on all sides. Remove meat to baking pan.

Add 2 Tablespoons oil to skillet. Add flour, stirring until browned. Gradually add beer and water. Cook and stir until sightly thickened. Stir in bouillon, bay leaf, sugar, thyme, basil and pepper. Pour over meat in baking pan. Cover baking pan with aluminum foil and bake for 2 hours or until beef is tender and gravy thickened. Remove bay leaf. Serve over hot noodles.

Serves 10

BRANDY CHICKEN IN CREAM

2 - 2 ½ lbs skinless chicken pieces
4 Tablespoons butter
2 cloves of garlic, split in half
6 Tablespoons brandy
1 cup heavy cream
1 Tablespoon curry powder
salt and pepper to taste
parsley, chopped
paprika

Cooked wide noodles

Preheat oven to 350 degrees.

In skillet, saute chicken and garlic in butter. Transfer to a casserole with juices from pan. Mix cream, brandy, curry powder and salt and pepper and pour over chicken. Cover and bake for 35-40 minutes. Sprinkle with finely chopped parsley and paprika.

Serve over a bed of wide noodles.

Serves 4

BEEF AND BROCCOLI STIR-FRY

1/4 cup soy sauce
1/4 cup dry sherry
1 Tablespoon honey
1 Tablespoon chopped garlic
2 tsp grated orange peel
1 lb flank steak, cut diagonally across grain into thin strips
1 large head broccoli, cut into florets
2 Tablespoons vegetable oil
1 Tablespoon cornstarch
salt and pepper
Cooked white rice

Whisk first 5 ingredients in large bowl. Add meat; toss to coat. Cover and refrigerate, 1 to 4 hours.

Blanch broccoli in large pot of boiling salted water 2 minutes. Drain. Rinse under cold water; drain well.

Heat oil in heavy large wok or skillet over high heat. Drain meat well, reserving marinade. Add cornstarch to reserved marinade and mix until smooth; set aside. Add meat to wok and stir-fry until almost cooked through, about 2 minutes. Add broccoli and stir-fry until crisp-tender, about 2 minutes. Add reserved marinade mixture and boil until sauce thickens and coasts meat and broccoli, stirring constantly, about 2 minutes. Season to taste with salt and pepper. Serve over rice.

4 servings

RUM-RUNNER CHICKEN

2 tsp oil

1 large onion, thinly sliced

6 garlic cloves, chopped

½ cup chicken broth

3 - 3 ½ lbs chicken pieces, cleaned, skinned

1/4 cup dark rum

2 Tablespoons apple cider vinegar

½ cup brown sugar, packed

½ tsp group cloves

½ tsp ground cinnamon

1/4 tsp group red pepper

1 tsp salt

Preheat oven to 350 degrees

In large skillet, heat the oil over medium heat. Stir in the onions and garlic and cook for 8 - 10 minutes or until golden. Remove from heat and stir in chicken broth. Pour into a 9 x 13 x 2 inch baking dish. Place chicken pieces over the top.

In medium bowl, combine remaining ingredients. Mix well to make a glaze. Brush half the glaze over the chicken and bake for 30 minutes. Drizzle the remaining glaze over the chicken and bake for 30 - 40 minutes or until no pink remains in the chicken.

Serves 3 - 4

BEEF STEW

½ cup flour

1/4 tsp pepper

1/4 tsp paprika

3 lbs beef chuck, cut into cubes

3 Tablespoons olive oil

1 small onion, dices

2 (12 oz) cans beer, room temperature

1 8-oz can tomato puree

1 Tablespoon brown sugar

1 tsp salt

1 bay leaf

2 celery stalks, chopped

4 carrots, chopped

4 russet potatoes, cut into cubes

1 cup frozen peas

In gallon-size plastic storage bag, mix flour, pepper and paprika. Add meat and shake to coat.

In large Dutch oven, heat olive oil. Brown meat in oil. Remove meat and set aside. Add chopped onions to pan and fry until brown.

Return meat to pan. Add beer, tomato puree, brown sugar, salt, and bay leaf. Stir to mix. Simmer, covered about 1 hour. Stir occasionally. Add potatoes carrots, and celery. Continue to simmer about 45 minutes. If additional liquid is needed during cooking, add more beer or water. Add peas and simmer additional 15 minutes.

Serves 8 - 10

CHICKEN MORNAY ON BROCCOLI

1 package frozen broccoli cuts (10oz)
1/4 cup butter
1/4 cup flour
1 cup chicken broth
½ cup heavy cream
½ cup dry white wine
salt and pepper to taste
1/4 tsp Worcestershire Sauce
1/3 cup plus 2 Tablespoons grated parmesan cheese
2 cups diced cooked chicken

Preheat oven to 425 degrees. In microwave or in saucepan on stove-top, cook broccoli until barely tender, drain and arrange in a shallow 1 ½ quart baking dish. In saucepan, melt butter and stir in flour. Add chicken broth and cream. Cook, stirring, until thickened. Stir in wine, salt and pepper. Add Worcestershire and 1/3 cup cheese.

Arrange chicken on broccoli, pour sauce over top and sprinkle with 2 Tablespoons cheese. Bake for 15 minutes, or until bubbly.

HONEY GLAZED MEATBALLS

1/4 cup onion, finely chopped
1 lb lean ground beef
3/4 cup fresh bread crumbs
1 egg, beaten
1 tsp salt
1/4 tsp pepper
1 Tablespoon flour
1 cup orange juice, room temperature
1 ½ Tablespoon lemon juice
1/4 cup Drambuie
1/4 cup honey
1 orange, sliced for garnish

Preheat oven to 350 degrees Spray 10 x 15 inch baking pan with non-stick cooking spray.

In large bowl, combine egg, salt, pepper, bread crumbs and onion. Mix well. Mix in ground beef. Shape into 24 1-inch meatballs. Place in baking pan.

In saucepan, blend flour with a small amount of orange juice. Over medium heat, gradually stir in the remaining orange juice, lemon juice, Drambuie, and honey. Bring to a boil, stirring constantly.
Brush meatballs with glaze. Bake for 25 minutes or until brown, brushing with remaining glaze twice during cooking. Garnish with orange slices.

OVEN-FRIED RUM CHICKEN

4 lbs chicken pieces, skinless
flour
1 can (13oz) evaporated milk
1/4 cup white rum
1 ½ cups seasoned bread crumbs
½ cup grated parmesan cheese

Preheat oven to 400 degrees. In bowl, mix milk and rum. On waxed paper, combine bread crumbs and cheese. Roll chicken pieces in flour, dip into milk mix. Roll in crumb mix. Place on greased baking sheet. Bake for 45 minutes.

ROUND STEAK IN BEER

2 lbs round steak
½ cup flour
1 large onion, sliced
1 (14.5 oz) can tomato puree
½ tsp oregano
1/4 tsp basil
1 tsp Worcestershire sauce
3/4 cup beer, room temperature
2 Tablespoons oil
salt and pepper to taste

Preheat oven to 350 degrees

In skillet heat oil. Dredge meat in the flour and then brown in the skillet. Place meat into a 2-qt casserole dish. In skillet, brown onion. Place onion on top of meat in casserole dish. To skillet, add tomatoes, oregano, basil, Worcestershire, beer, salt and pepper. Stir. Bring to a boil for 1 minute. Pour over meat. Cover and bake for 1 ½ hours.

Serves 4

COMPANY POT ROAST WITH MASHED POTATOES AND BLACK SAUCE

Beef

3 lbs beef short ribs

4 Tablespoons vegetable oil

1 cup carrots, peeled and chopped

1 cup celery, chopped

1 red onion, peeled and chopped

2 large bay leaves

5 sprigs flat-leaf parsley

1 ½ cups Zinfandel wine

4 cups unsalted beef stock

Black Sauce

4 cups Zinfandel

1 ½ cups packed dark brown sugar

3/4 cup raisins

Potatoes

1 ½ lbs Yukon Gold potatoes, un-peeled, quartered

1 ½ lbs russet potatoes, peeled, quartered

8 garlic cloves, peeled

1 Tablespoon salt

1 stick of butter

1 cup whipping cream

½ tsp black pepper

For ribs: In large, heavy Dutch oven, heat the oil. Sear the ribs on both sides until browned, about 3-4 minutes per side. Place the vegetables and herbs on top of the browned meat and add the wine. Bring to a boil and add enough stock to just cover the meat and vegetables. Bring to a boil. Reduce the heat to low and cover the pan. Braise the short ribs for 2-2 ½ hrs or until very tender.

For sauce: Combine vinegar and brown sugar in a saucepan. Bring to a boil. Reduce heat and simmer rapidly until reduce to 2 ½ cups, about 20-30 minutes. Add the raisins. Continue to reduce the sauce to 2 cups, about 10-15 minutes. Sauce should be very dark, syrupy and glassy. Be careful not to over-reduce the sauce, as it will burn quickly.

Let sauce cool slightly. Remove the raisins with a slotted spoon and reserve for garnish.

For potatoes: Combine potatoes and garlic in a large pan and add water to cover, plus 1 inch. Add the salt and bring to a boil. Lower heat and simmer 30-45 minutes until fork tender. Drain well. Add butter, cream, and pepper and mash with potato masher. Stir to smooth.

To Serve: Place a mound of the mashed potatoes on a plate, top with a de-boned short rib, and drizzle with the sauce. Garnish with the cooked raisins.

Serves 6-8

CHICKEN AND HAM ROLL-UPS

3 whole chicken breasts, split, skinned, boned (about 1 ½ lbs boneless)
6 slices boiled ham
2 Tablespoons olive oil
1 can cream of chicken soup
1/4 cup dry white wine

Place chicken between 2 sheets of waxed paper to flatten with flat side of knife. Remove waxed paper. Top each with slice of ham. Roll up. Secure with toothpicks. In skillet, brown roll-ups in olive oil. Stir in soup and wine. Cover. Cook over low heat for 20 minutes or until done. Stir occasionally.

Serves 6

APPLE BOURBON BAKED HAM

7-8 lbs fully cooked bone-in smoked ham
½ cup bourbon
1 ½ cups water
½ cup brown sugar, packed
½ cup apple cider
1/4 cup Dijon mustard
1 tsp pepper

Place unwrapped ham on rack in large roasting pan. Let stand at room temperature about 45 minutes. Preheat oven to 325 degrees.

Skin ham. Trim fat to 1/4 inch. Score fat in diamond pattern. Pour the water and 1/4 cup of the bourbon into roasting pan. Cover pan with foil. Bake 30 minutes.

Meanwhile, in small saucepan, combine 1/4 cup bourbon, the sugar and apple cider. Cook, stirring, over medium heat until sugar is dissolved. Remove from heat. Stir in mustard and pepper.

Baste ham with 1/4 of the glaze. Add water to pan, if needed.

Bake 1 ½ hour longer, basting 3 times with remaining glaze, or until internal temperature registers 140 degrees on meat thermometer. Let stand, tented with foil, for 15 minutes before slicing.

Serves 8 - 10

Breakfast Specials

He will fill your mouth with laughter and your lips with shouts of joy.

Job 8:21

GRAND MARNIER FRENCH TOAST WITH ORANGE RUM SAUCE

6 eggs, beaten
3/4 cup orange juice
1/4 cup Grand Marnier
1/3 cup milk
3 Tablespoons sugar
1 tsp vanilla
1/4 tsp salt
1 Tablespoon orange peel
Texas Toast size bread

1 stick butter
confectioners' sugar

In large bowl, combine eggs, orange juice, Grand Marnier, milk, sugar, vanilla, salt, and peel. Mix well. Melt a little of the butter on griddle or in skillet over medium-high heat. Dip bread into batter to coat both sides. Cook in butter until browned on bottom. Turn and brown other side. Remove to serving platter and sprinkle with confectioners' sugar. Serve immediately with orange rum sauce. Repeat to use all egg batter, heating additional butter for cooking, as needed.

Orange Rum Sauce:

1 cup sugar
2/3 cup orange juice
2 Tablespoons rum
1 Tablespoon Curacao
1 Tablespoon orange peel

In small saucepan, combine all ingredients. Bring to a boil over low heat, stirring constantly. Remove from heat. Let cool completely. Reheat to serve. Refrigerate leftovers.

KAHLUA PECAN WAFFLES

1 cup + 1 Tablespoon flour
½ tsp salt
2 Tablespoons sugar
2 3/4 tsp baking powder
½ tsp cinnamon
1/8 tsp ground nutmeg
1 stick butter, melted, cooled
2 eggs, separated, at room temperature
2 Tablespoons Kahlua
1 ½ cups milk, less 2 Tablespoons, at room temperature
1/3 cup chopped pecans

In large bowl, sift together all dry ingredients, except pecans. In another bowl, combine the egg yolks, butter, Kahlua, and milk. Whisk to mix. Whisk into flour mixture. And beat until smooth. Let batter rest for about 30 minutes. Beat egg whites until stiff, not dry. Fold egg whites and pecans gently into batter. Bake according to waffle iron directions.

BANANA CRUNCH FRENCH TOAST

1 cup maple syrup
1 oz dark rum
2 bananas, diced

8 thick slices bread (Texas toast size)
3 eggs
3/4 cup milk
½ tsp ground cinnamon
1 tsp vanilla
½ cup slice almonds - crushed
cooking oil
powdered sugar

In saucepan, stir together the maple syrup and rum. Bring to a boil over medium heat. Boil 1 minute. Remove from heat and add bananas. Let sit while preparing the french toast.

In medium bowl, combine eggs, milk, cinnamon and vanilla. Whisk well.

Heat griddle and add a small amount of cooking oil. Heat is right when a tiny drop of water dances across the griddle.
Dip, don't soak, each slice of bread in the egg batter. Place on griddle and sprinkle top with almonds. When underside is golden (peak under a corner), turn and cook the other side.

Place on warm serving plates and sprinkle with powdered sugar. Ladle rum glazed banana syrup over top.

KIRSCH AND DRIED CHERRY KUGELHUPF

(Alsatian breakfast yeast bread)

Cake:
1 cup dried tart cherries
½ cup golden raisins
4 Tablespoons kirsch

1/4 cup warm water (105-115 degrees)
Pinch of sugar
2 envelopes dry yeast
1 stick unsalted butter, room temperature
3/4 cup sugar
4 large egg yolks
1 Tablespoon grated lemon peel
2 tsp vanilla
1 tsp almond extract
1 tsp salt
1 tsp salt 3/4 cup lukewarm milk
3 ½ cups all-purpose flour

1 cup almonds, toasted, finely chopped

Glaze:
1 cup powdered sugar
2 tablespoons kirsch
2 tsp milk

For Cake: Combine first 3 ingredients in medium bowl. Let stand 15 minutes.

In small bowl, combine 1/4 cup warm water and pinch of sugar. Sprinkle yeast cover; stir to dissolve. Let stand 10 minutes.

Meanwhile, in large mixing bowl, beat 6 Tablespoons butter, 3/4 cup sugar, yolks, peel, vanilla, almond extract, and salt until well blended. Add yeast mixture, milk and 1 cup flour. Beat until smooth. Beat in dried fruits and their soaking liquid. Gradually add remaining 2 ½ cups flour and beat until very soft dough forms, about 6 minutes. Let stand 15 minutes.

Butter 12-cup kugelhupf or Bundt pan with 2 Tablespoons butter. Add almonds; tilt pan to coat bottom and sides. Spoon dough into pan. Cover with plastic and towel. Let dough rise in warm place until within 1 inch of top of pan, about 2 ½ hours.

Preheat oven to 350 degrees. Bake kugelhupf until tester inserted into center comes out clean, about 35 minutes. Let stand 10 minutes. Turn out onto rack; cool completely.

For Glaze: Combine sugar and kirsch in bowl. Add milk; stir. Spoon over kugelhupf.

FRENCH IRISH TOAST

1 loaf Texas Toast bread
4 eggs
1 Tablespoon Irish whiskey
1 ½ Tablespoons Irish cream liqueur
1 tsp vanilla
1/4 cup butter
confectioners' sugar for dusting

In large bowl, whisk together the eggs, Irish whiskey, Irish cream liqueur, and vanilla until well blended.

In skillet, heat 1 Tablespoon butter, over medium heat. Dip a slice of bread into the egg mixture to coat both sides - do not soak. Fry in the hot skillet until browned, turn and brown other side. Add more butter to skillet as needed. Sprinkle each slice with confectioners' sugar.

Index

Strawberry Spritzers 19

Sunny Champagne Punch 18

Breads

Amaretto Almond Muffins 43

Apricot Almond 42

Banana Crunch French Toast 185

Beer 33

Beer & Cheddar Muffins 33

Beer Dinner Rolls 40

Beer Puffs to Fill 36

Cranberry Citrus Muffins 39

French Irish Toast 186

Grand Marnier Cranberry Muffins 43

Grand Marnier French Toast
  w/Orange Rum Sauce 183

Irish Cream Muffins 31

Kahlua Pecan Waffles 184

Kirsch & Dried Cherry Kugelhupf 186-187

Kugelhupf 44

Maple Merlot 32

Pepper Cheese Beer 45

Rum Raisin Banana 35

Rum Raisin Carrot 41

Rye Beer 37

Sage & Cheese Beer 38

Whiskey Soda 34

Whole Wheat Beer 38

Cake

Black Forest 95

Bourbon Carrot 72

Bourbon Filling for cake 109

Brandy Apple Spice 61

Chocolate Mint 96

Cranberry Rum Coffeecake 86

Harvey Wallbanger 97

Kahlua Banana Coffeecake 94

Molten Spiced Chocolate Cabernet 65

Mud 100

Rum Raisin Ring 84

Tennessee Whiskey Fruitcake 98

Tiramisu 58-59

Chicken

Apple Wine 166

Brandy Chicken in Cream 171

Crepes 150

Grand Marnier 164

& Ham Rool-ups 179

Honey Pecan 168

Lemony 152

L'Orange 155

Mornay on Broccoli 175

Orange-Chile w/Black Beans 148

Oven-Fried Rum 177

Rum Runner Chicken 173

Tarragon 159

Teriyaki Chicken Wings 23

Cookies

Amarretto Brownies 60

Amaretto Butter 101

Biscotti 75

Black Forest Rugalach 82-83

Brandy Snaps 99

Cinnamon-Raisin Biscotti 90

Creme de Menthe Bars 73

Frosty Latte Bars 57

Grand Marnier Raisin Gingerbread Bars 63

Irish Cream Chocolate Chip 74

Irish Cream Sugar 79

Kourabiedes w/Cinnamon 76

Pina Colada Wedges 85

Rum Raisin Oatmeal 81

Sweet Pastry Squares 78

Custard

Brandied Caramel Flan 77

Kahlua Flan 80

Fish

Amaretto Salmon Oriental 169

Beer Batter Fish 152

Grilled Whiskey Salmon 166

Virginia Bay Scallops in Wine Sauce 147

Frosting

Cherry 87

Irish Cream 26, 111

Kahlua Glaze 111

Mocha 87

Orange 87

Peppermint Buttercream 111

Vanilla 87

Whiskey Glaze 106

Frozen Treats

Alexander Hummer 70

Chocolate Chip Hummer 70

Citrus Hummer 70

Cranberry Ice Cream Pie 91

Golden Hummer 70

Grasshopper Pie 57

Mint Hummer 70

Mocha Hummer 70

Pina Colada Wedges 85

Velvet Hummer 70

Watermelon Popsicles 66

Fruits

Amaretto Apples 92

Baked Bananas in Lemon-Rum Sauce 92

Bananas in Rum 69

Brandied Stuffed Dates 73

Chocolate Fondue 65

Grand Marnier Fruit Salad 25

Hazelnut Poached Pears 91

Poached Pear & Raspberry Trifle
w/Orange Custard 68

Sparkling Champagne Gelatin 102

Strawberry & Irish Cream Fool 83

Watermelon Popsicle 66

Fudge

Kahlua & Cream 93

Marinades

Bourbon Steak 116

Burgundy 117

Pie

Alexander 89

Apple Cranberry 66

Apple Wine 103

Black Bottom 93

Cherry Cordial 88

Grasshopper 67

Hershey Bar 71

Irish Cream 62

Margarita 64

Pork

Apple Bourbon Baked Ham 180

Chicken & Ham Roll-ups 179

Chipotle Orange Glazed Pork Chops 161

Drunken Spareribs 151
Ham-Beer-Grr... 157
Sesame Pork Appetizers 26
Tequila Pork Tenderloin 145

Soups
Apple-Beer Cheese 49
Corn Chowder 51
Cream of Broccoli 50
Potato Ham 53
Vegetable Cheese 52

Toppings
Amaretto Caramel Sauce 107
Balsamic Poppy Seed Dressing 119
Beer Cheese Dip 25
Beer Cheese Spread 24
Black Currant Sauce 110
Blueberry Sauce 110
Bourbon BBQ Sauce 117
Bourbon Glaze 72
Brandied Butterscotch Sauce 107
Brandy Butter Sauce 108
Brandy Peach Sauce 108
Cheese Balls 28
Chocolate Fondue 65
Chocolate Sauce 113
Cranberry and Port Sauce 119
Cranberry Honey Glaze 106
Orange Brandy Sauce 115
Orange-Plum Barbecue Sauce 118
Peach Jam Sauce 112
Pecan Bourbon Caramel Sauce 114
Plum Jam Sauce 113
Port Cheddar Cheese Spread 23
Portly Cranberry Sauce 112

Raisin Beer Sauce 106
Raspberry Grand Marnier Sauce 109
Raspberry Jam Sauce 114
Raspberry Rum Sauce 108
Red Wine Sweet Barbecue Sauce 118
Rum Glaze 84
Savory Cheese Spread 24
Sour Cherry Sauce 116
Strawberry Jam Sauce 115
Strawberry Champagne Sauce 110
Whiskey Glaze 106
White Chocolate Rum Sauce 107

Vegetables
Beer Battered 127
Marinated Medley 27

Asparagus
w/Beer & Honey Sauce 123

Beans
3-Bean Bourbon Bake 136
Beer Baked Beans & Franks 156
Black Beans & Rice w/Corn Salsa 128-129
Cowboy 130
Drunken Beans 124
Green Beans w/Garlic & Vodka 140

Broccoli
Cream Soup 50
in Wine Sauce 132

Carrots
Amaretto Almond 138
Bourbon 123
Bourbon Carrot Cake 62

Bourbon

3 Bean Bake 136

Apple Baked Ham 180

BBQ Sauce 117

Carrots 123

Carrot Cake 72

Drunken Spareribs 151

Filling 109

Glaze 72

Honey Pecan Chicken 168

Kentucky Sweet Potatoes 131

Mud Cake 100

Pecan Caramel Sauce 114

Pecan Smashed Sweet Potatoes 126

Steak Marinade 116

Yams w/Pecan Topping 125

Brandy

Acorn Squash 137

Alexander Hummer 70

Alexander Pie 89

Apple Cranberry Pie 66

Apple Spice Cake 61

Butter Sauce 108

Butterscotch Sauce 107

Caramel Flan 77

Cheese Balls 28

Chicken in Cream 171

Chocolate Fondue 65

Chocolate Chip Hummer 70

Cinnamon-Raisin Biscotti 90

Citrus Hummer 70

Fruit Punch 15

Kourabiedes w/Cinnamon Cookies 76

Orange Sauce 115

Peach Sauce 108

Pecan Carrots 141

Snaps 99

Stuffed Dates 73

Champagne

Deluxe Kir Royale 13

Kahlua Party Punch 16

Nectar Punch 14

Sparkling Gelatin 102

Sunny Punch 18

Strawberry Sauce 110

Coffee Liqueur

Banana Coffeecake 94

Chocolate Fondue 65

Chocolate Sauce 113

Frosty Latte Squares 57

Kahlua & Cream Fudge 93

Kahlua Flan 80

Kahlua Glaze 111

Kahlua Glazed Carrots 134

Kahlua Party Punch 16

Kahlua Pecan Waffles 184

Kahlua Picadillo 26

Mocha Hummer 70

Mocha Frosting 87

Peach Jam Sauce 112

Red Wine Sweet Barbecue Sauce 118

Tiramisu 58-59

Cognac

Blueberry Sauce 110

Shredded Beef Brisket 149

Cranberry Liqueur

Cranberry Punch 14

Creme de Cassis

Black Currant Sauce 110

Deluxe Kir Royale 13

Creme de Cacao

Alexander Hummer 70

Alexander Pie 89

Chocolate Chip Hummer 70

Golden Hummer 70

Grasshopper Pie 67

Hershey Bar Pie 71

Mint Hummer 70

Mocha Hummer 70

Velvet Hummer 70

Creme de Menthe

Bars 73

Chocolate Chip Hummer 70

Chocolate Mint Cake 96

Grasshopper Pie 67

Mint Hummer 70

Shake 13

Curacao

Fruit Punch 15

Drambuie

Honey Glazed Meatballs 176

Frangelico

Hazelnut Poached Pears 91

Galliano

Golden Hummer 70

Harvey Wallbanger Cake 97

Gin

Bathtub Gin Fizz 13

Grand Marnier

Appricot-Almond Bread 42

Black Forest Cake 95

Chicken 164

Chocolate Fondue 65

Cranberry Ice Cream Pie 91

Cranberry Muffins 43

French Toast 183

Fruit Salad 25

Orange Frosting 87

Orange Punch 15

Raisin Gingerbread Bars 63

Raspberry Sauce 109

Snow Peas 141

Strawberry Spritzer 19

Sweet Potatoes 135

Irish Cream Liqueur

Chocolate Chip Cookies 74

Chocolate Sauce 113

Creme de Menthe Shake 13

French Irish Toast 186

Frosting 26, 111

Sugar Cookies 79

Muffins 31

Pie 62

Strawberry Fool 83

Kirsch

Black Forest Cake 95

Black Forest Rugalach 82-83

Cherry Cordial Pie 88

Cherry Frosting 87

Chocolate Fondue 65
Dried Cherry Kugelhupf 185

Peach Schnapps
New Year's Cocktail 16

Peppermint Schnapps
Peppermint Buttercream Frosting 111
Peppermint-Rum Punch 17

Port
Beef Brisket w/Lemon Onion 163
Cranberry Sauce 119
Port Cheddar Cheese Spread 23
Portly Cranberry Sauce 112
Sour Cherry Sauce 116

Rum
Baked Bananas in Lemon-Rum Sauce 92
Banana Crunch French Toast 185
Bananas in Rum 69
Biscotti 75
Black Bottom Pie 93
Cranberry Citrus Muffins 39
Cranberry Coffeecake 86
Cranberry Honey Glaze 106
Cranberry Punch 14
Fruit Punch 15
Glaze 84
Grand Marnier French Toast
    w/Orange Rum Sauce 183
Hot Buttered Rum 14
Kugelhupf 44
Orange-Chile Chicken w/Black Beans 148
Oven Fried Chicken 177
Peach Jam Sauce 112

Peppermint-Rum Punch 17
Pina Colada Wedges 85
Plum Jam Sauce 113
Raisin Banana Bread 35
Raisin Carrot Bread 41
Raisin Oatmeal Cookies 81
Raisin Ring Cake 84
Raspberry Jam Sauce 114
Raspberry Rum Sauce 108
Rum Runner Chicken 173
Strawberry Jam Sauce 115
Tiramisu 58-59
White Chocolate Rum Sauce 107

Scotch Ale
Potatoes 139

Tequila
Chipotle Orange Glazed Pork Chops 161
Margarita Pie 64
Pork Tenderloin 145
Watermelon Popsicles 66

Triple Sec
Margarita Pie 64
Velvet Hummer 70

Whiskey
Glaze 106
French Irish Toast 187
Grilled Salmon 166
Soda Bread 34
Maple Glazed Carrots 130
Tennessee Whiskey Fruitcake 98
Tipsy Sweet Potatoes 137

Wine

Apple Chicken 166

Apple Pie 103

Baked Potatoes 127

Balsamic Poppy Seed Dressing 119

Beef Brisket w/Lemon Onion 163

Beef & Broccoli Stir Fry 172

Beef Burgundy 167

Black Beans & Rice w/Corn Salsa 128-129

Brisket in Sweet & Sour Sauce 165

Broccoli in Sauce 132

Burgundy Marinade 117

Chicken & Ham Roll-ups 179

Chicken Crepes 150

Chicken L'Orange 155

Chicken Mornay on Broccoli 175

Chicken Tarragon 159

Company Pot Roast 178-179

Corn Chowder 51

Cream of Broccoli Soup 50

Fruit Punch 15

Hot Spiced Wine 19

Lemony Chicken 152

Maple Merlot Bread 32

Marinated Vegetable Medley 27

Molten Spiced Chocolate Cabernet Cake 65

Orange-Plum Barbecue Sauce 118

Orange Punch 15

Plum Jam Sauce 113

Poached Pear & Raspberry Trifle
w/Orange Custard   68

Potato Ham Soup 53

Potato Salad 138

Roasted Garlic Mashed Potatoes 133

Sangria Spritzer 17

Savory Beef Brisket 156

Savory Cheese Spread 24

Sesame Pork Appetizers 26

Shallot Potato Salad 131

Shredded Beef Brisket in Wine 149

Slow Cooker Beef Bourguignonne 146

Slow Cooker Beef Pot Roast 160

Slow Cooker Beef Tips in Wine 162

Spaghetti w/Meat Sauce 154

Spiced Fruit Punch 18

Strawberry Jam Sauce 115

Strawberry Spritzer 19

Sunny Champagne Punch 18

Sweet Barbecue Sauce 118

Sweet Pastry Squares 78

Teriyaki Chicken Wings 23

Vodka

Green Beans w/Garlic 140

Harvey Wallbanger Cake 97

New Year's Cocktail 16